THE TURMERIC LATTE

M. Damodaran

As His Colleagues See Him

EXCEPTIONAL STORY OF EXEMPLARY LEADERSHIP

Curated by

DR DINESH TYAGI

PRABHAT
PRAKASHAN

Published by
PRABHAT PRAKASHAN PVT. LTD.
4/19 Asaf Ali Road,
New Delhi-110 002 (INDIA)
e-mail: prabhatbooks@gmail.com

ISBN 978-93-5562-641-7

THE TURMERIC LATTE: M. DAMODARAN AS HIS COLLEAGUES SEE HIM
Curated by Dr Dinesh Tyagi

Edition
First, 2024

Price
₹ 300 (Rupees Three Hundred Only)

Printed at
SS Japan Art, Delhi

Author's Note

During an interaction at Delhi University, when some young students were asked whether they would like to visit a Government office for various services, a resounding shout of "NO" echoed across the hall. The young audience had such pathetic experiences while visiting the government offices that hardly anyone appreciated the work being done by the civil services officers. Why is it that the Civil Services, which claim to produce sensitive, committed officers and change agents, are not respected or applauded by a vast majority of the population? Though Civil Service connotes all those who are Government servants but generally the term is used for three all India services (IAS, IPS,IFS), some Central Services (Revenue etc) and mainly for IAS as general public interface is with the department they are associated with. The Collector is considered as the "*Mai Baap*" by a large segment of the society and looked upon as an institution for resolving all the issues of citizens. His role is largely of a supervisor and support provider to other departments at the district level. Magisterial powers entrusted do provide extra credibility to the institution of Collector. However, Collector or District Magistrate is one assignment in the entire life of the civil servant. In fact most of the interface between the civil service with citizens takes place at various departments both at the Central and State levels. In the emerging society however, the term used for civil service is "*Babus*", which is derogatory and very often the civil servants are in the news for wrong reasons.

The new generation wants to join Civil services for social prestige, peer pressure, job security and of course the opportunity to "rule" over the vast population. There is no other service or job which offers the space to "boss over" mentor or support communities/citizens at such a young age. On the first day of the training at Mussoorie Academy, it is said that "you are the cream of the nation " and this message promotes arrogance, superiority complex and little or no respect for other services amongst a majority of the officers. Very few of course use the opportunity to really serve with passion, commitment and sincerity. Their zeal and passion continues at least in the initial 10-15 years (till they have field level postings). However the organization structure of the Government does restrict even such individuals as they progress in service. The hierarchical structure of only four classes (A to D), reflects the societal class structure and becomes an impediment to supporting the limited class of motivated civil service officers. A vast majority then treats the civil service as any other job and becomes self-serving rather than community serving.

Are there true leaders in the civil services who set examples for others? Most of the civil servants monger for self-praise, either through writing their own biography or delivering talks/lectures about what they did in service. How the civil servant "fought" with political bosses inculcates the "hero" model of civil servants. There is a class which thrives on its own laurel. Some of them, however, are also remembered by the public and the community for the excellent work they seem to have done in that job/ area. Leadership is however different as these individuals are team builders, exceptional motivators, risk takers and passionate with the ability to perform under any circumstances, and are always prepared to work and deliver under difficult circumstances. They never take credit for the work and always assign to the team, but take full responsibility for anything which has gone wrong or not on expected lines. They are remembered in every institution they have worked in, and for the people who have worked with them, they become a role model. These are the true leaders within the Civil Services, though they are very rare. They are the unsung heroes and largely live in oblivion as they do not publish their autobiographies. For them it is simply "service" to the nation.

I propose to highlight about one such true leader - an institution builder and a great motivator - Mr M Damodaran, a 1971 batch IAS officer of erstwhile Manipur-Tripura cadre. He has worked in the State Government of Tripura, in the Central Government in different capacities and has left an indelible mark in each institution he worked in. He was given the charge of Indian bank as CMD when the bank was in serious trouble and many experts were suggesting its closure. He was then assigned the responsibility to restructure UTI when the institution was in deep trouble due to various stock market scams. He was also asked to ensure a smooth merger of IDBI(development financial institution) with IDBI bank. In his last assignment with the Government, as SEBI chief (chairman), he brought structural reforms to ensure the investor's confidence and made the system more transparent and accountable. Even after retirement when there were issues amongst Indigo promoters, he was inducted as chairman of the Board to resolve the differences. In every institution where Mr Damodaran worked, he is considered by many officers as their "Role Model."

This book is a collection of the events, episodes and personal experiences of officers who have worked with Mr Damodaran and how he influenced their life and brought significant transformation in the institutions he worked with. This is also an attempt to share the amazing and fascinating stories told by colleagues about Mr Damodaran's leadership and other qualities which are worth emulating by the young civil service officers.

I have spoken to Mr Damodaran and requested him to write his autobiography but he has always been reluctant as he believes that such biography generally leads to self-praise which is not good for a civil servant. He believes that for a civil servant the work should speak and he / she should always be in oblivion. The experiences and qualities which Mr Damodaran possesses as an individual and as a civil servant need to be shared with others, especially with future generations of civil servants. So some of us who worked with him decided to write about him and publish this book.

I must acknowledge the contribution of all the reputed persons from respected fields who consented to write about Mr Damodaran, despite the fact that many of them have retired and perhaps had to write and share without any help (steno). I am sure that despite the logistical difficulties, everyone wanted to share the memorable incidents/ anecdotes arising out of their association and working with Mr Damodaran. One chapter is written by a young girl who worked with Mr Damodran for a considerable long period after his retirement.

I must thank Mrs Damodaran on behalf of all the contributors of the book, all of whom shall always remember the hospitality, love and affection she has shown to Mr Damodarn's colleagues and continues to extend even after they are no longer associated with him in official capacity.

I also acknowledge the support provided by my daughter Richika in completing the compilation and editing of this book. She has given valuable inputs in designing the cover and title of the book.

❑

Contents

Chapter 1

Mr Damodaran - A Professional Thinker and An Institution Builder

– Dr Dinesh Tyagi
Retd IAS

A meeting was organised by the Ministry of Finance, Government of India to discuss various issues regarding the banking sector in the year 2001. The RBI Governor was also present. As usual, notes prepared by the Finance Ministry were circulated among the participants (Public sector banks, RBI and the Finance Ministry officials). Among the notes there were some "out of the box" thinking notes prepared—proposal to set up a "holding" company for all the public sector banks and for addressing the issues of NPA in banks. There was a suggestion to promote Asset reconstruction companies, where the NPA of banks could be transferred on mutually agreed terms and conditions. Dealing with bank assets even if they are classified as NPA by outside agencies was at that time not even thought of since it would give an impression that the fault/responsibility of banks for NPA was being diluted or shifted. There was also a feeling in some sections of the regulator/ Government that the role of the investigating agencies will not be there once the NPA are taken out of the books of the banks. This apparently appeared to be diluting accountability and responsibility for the bad assets of the banks. However, the note by the Ministry was based on sound and logical bank practices for improving the health of the bank and thereby not impinging on their potential to lend to the various sectors, as it was essential for the economic growth. The Joint secretary responsible for this was Mr Damodaran who was always thinking out of the box and suggesting measures for the long term strategy for strengthening the banking sector in India. He was called by the RBI Governor who appreciated the note circulated by the Ministry about promoting ARC as well as for the Holding company for PSB. During the meeting itself, Mr Damodaran called me, introduced me to the Governor and mentioned that the notes on ARC and Holding company were prepared by me. I was Director in the Ministry and was working under him. *Extending credit to subordinates for the good work is a rare quality of Mr Damodaran.*

Highly Persuasive

The Government of India was very concerned about the health of the banking sector especially after the Harshad Mehta scam (Security scam) and large scale NPA reported by some banks. Various measures were being taken by the regulator including stricter enforcement of the prudential norms, redefining asset classification and provisioning norms, prompt corrective action, narrow banking (restricting new asset creation) under certain circumstances. The Indian banking being predominantly public sector, the focus was also to improve the Governance in public sector banks. Mr Damodaran was in-charge of suggesting measures to improve the Governance structure in PSBs. He invited the three directors on the Board of the weak PSB (JS level officers were getting appointed as Government nominee directors on the strong / good banks and director levels on the weak bank while in actual practice it should have been the reverse). He asked each of the directors for suggestions for improving the weak banks. Among others, one of the suggestions was to reconstitute the Board and get CMD appointed from outside the state. Generally a person from the same state (where the bank was headquartered) was appointed by the Government as CMD like a Tamil person in an Indian bank, a Bengali in UBI, UCO or Allahabad bank and a Sikh in Punjab and Sind bank. The fact that this practice could be reviewed and modified was almost unthinkable due to the political and other regional pressure groups prevailing at that time. It was Mr Damodaran who could get this done due to his persuasive and convincing abilities. For the first time the Government appointed CMD from outside the "State" for these weak banks and it turned out to be instrumental in the revival of the banks. Incidentally, some outside expert committee had recommended the closure of these banks. Mr Damodaran had skills of convincing both at the RBI and the Executive/ Political levels as well as the PMO for making such significant changes. When he is convinced that it is in the best interest of the institution, he will meet and persuade everyone to extend support. He is a go-getter and never loses hope even in the most difficult situations.

Public sector banks have a peculiar culture that when there is promotion envisaged for some officer, a large number of complaints will start – either by those in the ranks who want to avoid competition or supersede or by other interested parties, intermediaries and Unions. As is the practice, once there is a complaint, the vigilance clearance to the concerned officer is not given by the Ministry. Sometimes genuine outstanding officers suffer due to this practice. In one case the complaint about an officer of a bank due for promotion as CMD was sent to CBI for investigation. CBI was not giving the clearance. Knowing the officer was very honest and no malafide could be assigned to him, Mr Damodaran, who was the CVO in the Ministry, went to meet the officer in charge in the CBI, an SP rank officer (Being the Director of Vigilance, I accompanied him). Generally no JS level officer in government will do such follow up for others. He appreciated the SP's work and investigation skills and thereafter told him that this banker has not even taken a pencil home from the bank for personal purpose and his integrity was beyond doubt. It was only because of Mr Damodaran's persuasive skills that the SP in CBI could be convinced and he sent a report which exonerated the banker who became CMD of a large bank and later the chairman of BIFR. This quality of helping those who do not have "*Mai baap* " in the system is a very rare asset of Mr Damodaran. Later, one day the banker in question came to the office with tears in his eyes and said "I have never met you or spoken to you, yet you helped me. It must be God's will." I did mention to him that it was Mr Damodaran who fought for him and saw to it that people with integrity are protected and supported.

Unique Risk Taking Ability

When I joined the Banking division in the Ministry of finance, my reporting boss, JS told me that the officer before me was very intelligent and had taught in Harvard. However, he did not work to my satisfaction and his two year ACR was in the Almirah (at one corner of the room). The Almirah was kept flooded with papers which was very unusual for an officer of his rank. Once he misbehaved with me as it was his general tendency to bully subordinates and I told him "you can write whatever you want in my ACR but next time do not misbehave". He asked me to report to the secretary and get a change in the work allocation. I told him that if he did not like or was not satisfied, he should ask for a replacement. This officer always made changes with 'pencil" on any note prepared by the subordinate and later when the fair copy was put up, he would remove the draft or erase the pencil marks made by him. He later became secretary to the Government of India. In contrast Mr Damodaran has been a leader in the true sense – supporting, encouraging and protecting the subordinates. I do not think he ever misbehaved with any one during his entire career, especially the subordinates. For him, building a team, guiding the new generation of civil services officers and doing the assigned work with great passion was the norm and he never bothered about his own or shirked from taking risk and responsibility.

Always Helpful and Supportive

Once I was called by the Chief Minister to the office on a Holiday. This was unusual in Tripura. He was annoyed as I had told him that it was "unfair" not to approve my station leave during the "Puja Holidays." He told me "You can look for a job elsewhere." This happened in the presence of the then Chief Secretary who did not even try to console me after the unwarranted misbehaviour of the CM. I applied for three months leave which was sanctioned. I met Mr Damodaran who was posted at that time in Delhi and told him about the incident with the CM. He asked me to meet the chairman IL&FS as they were looking for an IAS officer for a project with the Ministry of Electronics and IT. I then joined IL&FS for the CSC project implementation in the year 2006 and later resigned from IAS in the year 2008 as the CSC project provided me the opportunity to build and promote rural entrepreneurship and support rural citizens in getting access to Government services close to their residence. Mr Damodaran has always been very helpful and has supported all those who worked with him - a rare quality of a great leader in the civil services.

I have just completed my tenure in Government of India in the Ministry of finance which included more than two years as custodian of Harshad Mehta Scam (Securities Scam 1992). This assignment provided an opportunity to manage assets and dispose of them within the legal constraints. All the Assets in the case were to be disposed of with the approval of the Special Court (almost all the assets of Harshad Mehta and associates, which were pending since 1992, were disposed of). The Special court Judge at Mumbai (who later became the Chief Justice Of Supreme Court) told me that he would speak to the PMO for my retention as Custodian as I had promised to close the custodian office within the next two years – dispose of all the assets and distribute them to the stakeholders (unfortunately the office still continues). Mr Damodaran in the meantime joined as the Chairman of IDBI and was assigned the work of merger of the IDBI with IDBI bank. In order to address the issue of NPA in the IDBI bank, an ARC was set up. Mr Damodaran sent an offer to me to join as the Executive Director in IDBI to work as CEO of the ARC. I was very excited and requested the State Government for permission. This, incidentally, was the same State Government which had asked me to look for a job elsewhere a year after. However, they did not give me permission. The Chief Secretary did not even support. (He was an officer who looked after only his own interest and did not bother about the subordinates).

Once while working in the State, I got the news of the sudden demise of my elder brother in a Hospital where he was looking after my mother who was suffering from cancer. Mr Damodaran was the Chief Secretary. He sent two other officers to my house who booked my ticket and arranged for all that was required to reach Delhi (where my family lived). After staying in Delhi for a few days, I informed Mr Damodaran that though I had not applied for any formal leave, I would like to stay for one month to look after my ailing mother. He told me " Do not bother, we will regularize everything. You look after your mother." Mr Damodaran always supports his colleagues even in matters which may not be purely official and that is why everyone who has ever worked under him has developed a relationship with him irrespective of wherever they might have later gone for work. His love, caring nature and unstinted support motivates the young ones and enables them to perform to the best of their ability in the interest of the organization/

institution they serve. In contrast there was an officer for whom the IAS association in the State protested to the Chief Minister and opposed the bringing of an officer from outside the State as Chief Secretary. Later, he was made Chief secretary, initially to be tried for three months, as we were told by the then CM that he was not considered suitable because of his performance in his previous jobs in the State. This officer then continued for more than 7 years as CS which was a record in Tripura. As Secretary he lobbied to get a District Magistrate's job which he missed as he had left the State and gone to the central government as under-secretary. This Chief Secretary wrote in my Annual confidential report that "the officer is more interested in personnel matters than official." He also made similar comments like "he does not keep good health" about an outstanding officer who was rated one of the best by none other than Mr S R Shankaran (an Andhra cadre officer and Secretary Rural Development) - a role model for most of the Tripura cadre officers. Incidentally Mr Shankaran on deputation was chief secretary of Tripura, an institution and a rare breed of officers in civil services (he stayed in guest house for five years, handled the1980 Tripura riots and inculcated the pride and honour in the officers who were allotted the Tripura cadre)

Fearless and Firm

While working as Joint Secretary in the Information and Broadcasting Ministry, one day Mr Damodaran got a call (which his wife received) from someone who spoke in Punjabi initially, threatening them "leave Delhi and go back to state or the consequences will be bad". On informing the police, he was offered a police picket in front of his house but he politely refused. On inquiry later, it was found that the call was made from the room of the Secretary (I&B) who incidentally was also not happy about some of the decisions being taken by him. Mr Damodaran is a fearless person and was neither scared nor could be bullied by any one - be it from an official or political level.

Mr Damodaran to me personally has been a mentor, guide and a leader whom you can look up to when in problem or doubt. His style of working, passion, hard work and team building efforts are exemplary for the new generation of civil servants.

❑

Chapter 2

His Tenure in Banking Division - Ministry of Finance

– Dr K Cherian Varghese

Former Chairman: BIFR/ Union Bank of India

April 6, 1970 was a special day in the life of a small group of aspiring young Indians. They met at the Indian Bank Staff College at Adayar in Madras (now Chennai) -- the first batch of Probationary Officers selected by Indian Bank after its nationalization. The group included M Damodaran who later joined IAS. I sat next to him in the class of young bank probationers. My association with Mr Damodaran is since the time he got his first job - a young man full of zeal and passion.

The excitement resulting from the "nationalization of 14 major banks" announced by the late Prime Minister of India, Mrs Indira Gandhi, was still fresh in the air and filled a large section of the Indian populace with hope and aspiration. Earlier, before nationalization, the commercial banking system in India was predominantly in the private sector. The large banks had been extending financial assistance mostly to trade and industry owned by the influential and privileged people. Connection with the groups which controlled the banking institutions helped business entities to get loans easily and on attractive terms.

However small business, traders and merchants largely depended on private money lenders for finance. Access to banking services was not easily available to small businesses, agriculture and the common man as these segments/sectors were not a priority for the banking system which was dominated by the big banks in the private sector. The Social Control of Banks initiated in 1968 by the Government of India could not meet the expectations from the big commercial banks which served mainly the elite. Banking services were not available in the rural and semi urban areas. Even urban areas had a very limited number of branches. It was unimaginable to get a job in a commercial bank for those who had no connections with the owners or the management. In this context, nationalization of 14 major banks with total deposits of Rs.50 crore and above was announced by the Government of India on 19th July, 1969 by an ordinance. Indian Bank was one of them - the banks nationalised. These banks accounted for 85 percent of the deposits of the banking system. The Banking Companies (Acquisition and Transfer of Undertaking) Act, 1970 was passed by the Parliament with retrospective effect from 19th July, 1969. The Act was: "to provide for the acquisition and transfer of certain banking companies, with regard to their size, resources, coverage and organization, in order to control the heights of the economy and to meet progressively, and serve the needs of development of the economy in conformity with national policy and objectives and for matters connected therewith or incidental thereto."

The nationalized banks started advertising for recruitment. People expected that the nationalized banks would play a pivotal role in the economic development of the nation and would be an important instrument for social transformation by offering their services to the hitherto neglected sections of society and even geographically disadvantaged locations. A large number of young people were eager to join the banking sector which started offering placements through a transparent and merit based recruitment process. They were excited by the prospect of being part of the noble effort of nation building apart from getting a remunerative job as these banks offered relatively higher salaries. They also aspired to provide leadership in the financial sector to bring about social change.

The three week long training program at the Staff College of Indian Bank was to induct the new entrants for the great tasks ahead. After the induction program they were to get on the job training for a period of two years at different branches of the bank before confirmation as officers.

Ability to Think Differently and Articulate Effectively

We were introduced to the basics of banking at the Staff College. Towards the end of the training program each one was asked to speak in the class on a topic of his choice. Three of us were rated as the toppers in public speaking. All three of us went on to head banking institutions later in our career. Damodaran who was among the three spoke on "realism in Indian cinemas." The predominant view at that time was that cinemas should be based on realistic stories. Damodaran successfully argued that cinema is a work of art where creativity and imagination should be allowed a free hand. It was evident that he could think differently, had an opinion of his own, and was efficient in communicating his views to others.

A Person Who Always Found Goodness in Others

The nationalized banks were headed by a Custodian who was later designated as the Chairman and Managing Director. G Lakshminarayanan, the well-respected Custodian of Indian Bank addressed the officers on the last day of the induction program. While emphasizing the need to be good to people wherever we were posted, he narrated a story. "In the olden days when there were no hotels, a traveller reached a village at sunset. He asked a villager, "Can you please suggest the name of a good person with whom I can stay overnight?" The villager asked: 'Are you a good person? If you are a good person everyone in this village will be good to you.' This in retrospect characterizes Mr Damodaran - a person who always found goodness in others. We were posted to different branches of Indian Bank and left the college with a pledge to be good to others.

After about six months, Damodaran left Indian Bank and joined State Bank of India as a Probationary Officer. Later he entered the Indian Administrative Service. The foundation for his future role in the financial sector must have been well laid during his initial training in the two banks. He went on to become Chief Secretary to the Government of Tripura.

We met again when he was posted as Joint Secretary in the Banking Division of the Government of India in New Delhi. During his tenure in the Banking Division he established a reputation for his clarity of thought, quick grasping power, helpful nature and ability to stand up for justice. These qualities endeared him to the banking fraternity. On completion of his stint in the Banking Division he took up an assignment with Reserve Bank of India with his base at New Delhi. Organizing the rehabilitation of the then ailing banks like Indian Bank and UCO Bank was part of his new role. He also acted as Chairman and Managing Director (CMD) of Indian Bank for a while until a regular CMD was posted.

Unit Trust of India is the oldest Mutual Fund in India. It was also the largest Mutual Fund till 2000. UTI was a large investor in the stock market. It also acted as a promoter of institutions like the UTI Bank (renamed Axis Bank), made strategic investments in large companies and made equity contributions in unlisted companies, as a means to promote new business enterprises. Retail investors as well as financial institutions had been reposing trust in UTI. It had a significant role in promoting savings and capital formation in the country. It went through ups and downs during different periods. UTI was an institution of systemic importance for the financial sector. Banks used to invest their surplus funds in the flagship US-64 Scheme of the UTI. At the beginning of every month the sale and repurchase price of the units in US-64 used to be announced by UTI. The US-64 Scheme offered good liquidity also as the units could be tendered for repurchase to UTI. There was no regulatory oversight over UTI by the Securities and Exchange Board of India (SEBI) as it was formed under a separate legislation. The basis of stipulating the sale and repurchase price of units under the US-64 that was valid for a month was not known to the investors.

A Rescue Man - Whose Mere Appointment Could Build Investor Confidence

In 2001 while on a flight from Mumbai to Mangalore, the headquarters of Corporation Bank, I read a news item in the Economic Times about the US-64 Scheme having serious problems. Immediately after reaching the office, as Chairman and Managing Director of Corporation Bank, I asked the Investment Department of the bank to divest the bank's large investment in the US-64 Scheme. The head of the Investment Department argued against divesting the US-64 as this scheme of UTI was considered a very sound and remunerative investment. He had so much confidence in UTI from his past experience. I had picked up the warning signals, and ordered the immediate exit from the US-64 Scheme. The bank could get out of the investment well in time without any loss. Perhaps many other investors including the very large ones might have ignored the early news items. Soon more and more alarming reports started to come out. UTI was in serious trouble. Sale and repurchase of US-64 units was suspended. Anxiety and panic was palpable in the financial sector. It was a full blown crisis. As an institution of systemic significance, UTI had to be rescued. Damodaran was picked up by the Government of India to rebuild/revive UTI, and was appointed as its Chairman in 2001.

Damodaran was already well known in the banking sector. His appointment as Chairman of UTI came as a relief and confidence building measure especially for the small investors including the institutional ones. Backing of the Government of India and Damodaran's acceptability to the large investors calmed the situation as the institution was really in turmoil. He started his mission with clarity of thought and strategic intent. Damodaran got the large investments of the US-64 Scheme in promoted institutions, illiquid investments in unlisted companies and guaranteed schemes which offered specified returns transferred to the Specialized Undertaking for Unit Trust of India (SUUTI) created by the Government of India. The UTI Act got repealed and UTI also was put under the regulatory oversight of SEBI. UTI was thus able to pay undivided attention to its mutual fund role. Investors were back at UTI with their old mutual fund. Damodaran's mission was hailed as a successful turnaround story in the financial sector.

Rebuilding the Industrial Development Bank of India (IDBI) was the next mission for Damodaran. In 2003 he was appointed as the Chairman of IDBI. As a development financial institution, IDBI had played a significant role in the industrial development of India. IDBI was established under the Industrial Development Bank of India Act, 1964. There was hardly any large industrial project in which IDBI was not a participant. Most of the time, it was the lead institution. When new banking licences were issued by the Reserve Bank of India, IDBI had promoted the IDBI Bank to do commercial and retail banking. IDBI as a development financial institution had large stressed assets accumulated over the years. On the liabilities side IDBI had high cost long term debentures issued with fixed interest rates. These were big challenges. Under Damodaran's initiative the problem loans were transferred to SASF (Stressed Assets Stabilisation Fund). The IDBI Act was repealed. IDBI Bank was merged with IDBI and the new entity IDBI Bank Ltd was formed which facilitated access to less expensive customer deposits.

In February, 2005 Damodaran was appointed as the Chairman of Securities and Exchange Board of India (SEBI), the market regulator. With his experience in UTI and familiarity with the financial sector, he initiated steps for improving corporate governance as a priority and became a vocal spokesperson on the topic. He also paid attention to the development of education in the area of the securities market. National Institute of Securities Markets (NISM) was an institution which was dear to his heart. He ensured that the Board of Governors of NISM included people with experience in the corporate world and the financial sector. On his invitation I also had the opportunity to serve on the Board of Governors of NISM.

Damodaran made an indelible mark on the institutions where he served and the people he worked with. For the financial sector, his contribution will always be remembered and his leadership remains inspiring to the budding aspirants in this sector.

❑

Chapter 3

The UTI Revival— An Untold Story

– Rehman Imtaiyazur

In our professional sojourn, we all witness diligent and challenging circumstances. Occasionally, some of us are presented with an absolutely unprecedented defiance /demand. Something similar happened on 15th July 2001, when Mr Damodaran was entrusted with the responsibility of taking charge of the erstwhile Unit Trust of India as its Chairman. It was amidst diverse challenges that the institution was facing and the general uncertainties in the financial sector during that period.

When I reflect upon the career achievements of Mr Damodaran, one that shines bright like a north star is his breath-taking tenure at UTI. As a member of the UTI family, I was fortunate enough to work and interact closely with Mr Damodaran, trying to learn and imbibe some of his exceptional qualities. At UTI, Mr. Damodaran demonstrated his strong administrative prowess, decisiveness and ability to manage difficult situations, thus establishing himself as the "turnaround man." His accomplishments in turning around the institution soon became a legend for numerous business case studies.

For me, these events and their successful outcomes – restructuring of the erstwhile UTI, creation of the SEBI-registered UTI Asset Management Co. Ltd., my appointment as the first company secretary of UTI AMC, the mentorship and empowerment that Mr Damodaran bestowed upon me and the opportunity to manage challenging situations – have been inflection points that created a new direction in my life, positively impacting my own professional career.

Establishing Himself as A Leader in New field

I am reminded of July 2001, when Mr Damodaran – who was a Joint Secretary in the Ministry of Finance and an OSD (Officer on Special Duty) at the Reserve Bank of India based at New Delhi – was given a new assignment as Chairman of UTI in Mumbai. After taking charge at UTI, his first-ever address to the employees, at its corporate office in New Marine Lines, showcased his dynamic leadership, confidence, clarity of thought and extraordinary oratory skills. This instantly boosted the morale of employees and evoked admiration and trust for their new leader, whose immediate task was to navigate the organisation out of its crisis situation. His strong record in the Banking Division of the Ministry of Finance and in nursing back the health of weak banks during his short stint in the RBI was already well known. UTI for him was new and he had never worked with a mutual fund or in the capital market. During the first meeting itself, he could establish a rapport with the employees who could see clarity in his approach, thought and direction. This is one of the rare qualities he possesses - he can quickly establish himself even in unknown territories.

Restructuring and Creating a New UTI

At UTI, The immediate task for Mr Damodaran was to arrange the required financial liquidity to meet the requirements of scheme redemptions, restore investors' confidence, maintain the credibility of the institution and prevent any possible systemic risk in the financial sector – a task which he managed extremely well while making it seem effortless. It was not easy given the circumstances - financial scams and investor confidence at its lowest. Being vulnerable to rumours, it was important to restore the faith and trust of the investors to avoid a complete run on withdrawals. This was also serious as it was impinging on the financial sector as a whole. His communication to all the stakeholders helped in restoring the confidence and prevented the immediate crisis of liquidity to meet the obligation of payment to investors willing to withdraw/ redeem.

The next task was that of fulfilling the Government's objective of having a long-term solution for enabling de-risking of the Government from the business activities of UTI. Working closely with the Government, he played a major role in enacting the UTI Repeal Act 2002, bifurcating the erstwhile UTI into SUUTI, a government-owned body and UTI Mutual Fund, a SEBI-registered entity, and identifying shareholders for the Asset Management Company in a manner that communicated to the investors at large that UTI AMC is sponsored by four large and strong financial institutions, viz. SBI, LIC, PNB and BOB.

As the Chairman & Managing Director of UTI AMC as well as the Administrator of SUUTI, he did a stellar job in segregating the assets and liabilities of the erstwhile UTI into the two newly-formed institutions and putting in place processes and a governance system for the independent working of these two organisations. I have seen the meticulous manner in which each aspect of the business operation, including the bifurcation of accounting and finance functions due to the vesting of assets/ liabilities between the two organisations, was completed with precision. The task was humongous and, as part of the finance team, it was a once-in-a-lifetime experience for me.

Mr Damodaran had the unique opportunity and challenge of managing the largest restructuring exercise in the Indian financial sector. When he left UTI AMC in 2004, it was the largest, most well-run and respected AMC in the industry.

A Leader With Extraordinary Qualities—Believed in Empowering People

In the ensuing days, weeks and months, people at UTI had the opportunity of discovering him as an amiable person and a hard task master. He was in full control of his actions and emotions. Forthright in speaking up, decisive and a social person with inner strength, Mr Damodaran believed in empowering people. He was a man of few words and avoided meaningless discussions as he did not have the luxury of time, given the magnitude of issues he had to resolve in a very short period of time. But the words he spoke hit the chord right with power and impact. I have also witnessed him working in silence, across different areas involving complex business matters at UTI and performing multiple tasks in quick succession. The speed with which he could grasp issues and deftly manage the multiple stakeholders and boards of which he was a member, was just stunning for me to witness from close quarters. There is so much to learn merely by seeing him functioning, conducting meetings, dealing with political bosses and important personalities. I believe all those who worked with him or associated with him in official capacity to be fortunate.

Amidst all this, he still took time out to watch his favourite sport - Football. While people in leadership roles have capabilities and personalities somewhat similar to each other, some of the qualities that Mr Damodaran exhibited have been unique, and this is what makes him stand out, drawing admiration from peers and subordinates alike. These are qualities that one so admires, reveres, but finds it difficult to emulate.

Delinking the Roles of the CEO and CIO

Mr Damodaran had a clear idea of his own role as the CEO. As he mentioned, he aimed to "stay away from investment decisions" and to leave those in the hands of "a group of professionals." The CEO, according to him, should confine his job to make sure that "the investments don't go out of line with the overall philosophy of the organisation, which promises safe returns to the ordinary investor."

Accordingly, he delinked the CEO's role from that of the CIO. Although he was monitoring the investment decisions, Mr Damodaran did not take part in the buying and selling decisions, which were left to professional fund managers. He remarked, "The fact that the CEO is not the CIO demonstrates that the investment function is in the hands of a specialist who knows his job, who has to do that job and nothing else. He doesn't have to run the organisation." This distinction empowered the CIO whose focus was to only look after the interest of the investor and thus it helped in restoring the confidence of the large community of investors in UTI - and even new investors participated in large numbers.

Recognizing Talent and Creating Environment to Flourish

Mr Damodaran believed that "UTI insiders had what it took to restore the organisation to health and strength, provided an enabling environment was created." He had said this in a media interview: "I think it's due to the systems put in place, putting the right people in the right job. It's the result of having much more transparency, increased disclosures and addressing several legacy issues and recognizing that this is an organisation with an enormous storehouse of talent. It is not that the talent has appeared overnight, it's been there. Allowing them to excel themselves has been one of the key things in the transformation."

Mr Damodaran had also mentioned: "Key to the turnaround exercise was the restoration of employee morale and self-belief enabling a large number of them to rise to unexpected heights of performance." For the first time in UTI, he introduced incentivisation of employees by way of variable compensation schemes to attract and retain talent. It goes to the credit of Mr Damodaran and UTI's internal team that such a restructuring exercise in the Indian financial sector took place seamlessly - a case study for management schools.

Having the Right Process and Technology

As UTI Mutual Fund commenced its business as a SEBI-registered mutual fund on 1st February 2003, he led the team to set out new guidelines and operating procedures in conformity with SEBI's regulations. He also took the initiative to introduce a Front Office for the execution of investment deals with appropriate systems for adhering to regulatory guidelines. Thereby, fund managers were enabled to focus on managing their schemes while other activities were taken care of by technology.

At that time, since multiple computer applications were causing delays in the accounting functions, he approved a new and efficient MFund system in place of the earlier SAP system, which introduced tremendous efficiency and speed in the system and the NAV calculation process. Simplification, ease of functioning and compliance were his priority and he promoted the use of technology to address all these issues.

Governance and Transparency—Key to Reform

Transparency was the watchword in all his actions as he had to regain the confidence of the small investors. He put in place operations and systems to promote efficiency and accountability. His measures on teamwork and building shared ownership of issues created a vibrant organisation - UTI AMC.

Given his long experience with the government and deep understanding of governance issues, he was able to effectively address and resolve matters related to Board Governance and Shareholders' issues. He brought major transformation in governance, investment philosophy, risk mitigation practices and disclosure norms. Mr Damodaran continued to remain committed to corporate governance and transparency issues and, much later, in an interview, he asserted, "As they say – sunlight is the best disinfectant, the more things come out in the open, the better."

The Emergence of UTI AMC As A Professional, Board-Governed Asset Manager

Mr Damodaran created the Vision and Mission statement for UTI AMC. Contrary to perceptions, UTI AMC grew in strength and went on to make an acquisition of its own. In 2004, UTI AMC bought out the schemes of IL&FS Mutual Fund. On being asked whether inorganic growth would now be the way, he replied "No, organic growth will be our preferred way. Takeovers would, at best, supplement it."

Today, two decades after the restructuring, UTI AMC has evolved as a listed, professional and Board-governed asset management institution with a much-enhanced standard of governance and transparency. Its operations include domestic mutual funds, portfolio management services, offshore business, retirement solutions and Alternate Investment Business. As UTI remains committed to the objectives for which it was founded, this institution is also grateful to its past leaders, such as Mr Damodaran, for laying a strong foundation and creating a rich legacy for the institution to continue operations.

If Mr Damodaran has achieved remarkable progress in UTI, it is because of his competence, honesty and sincerity. Being a visionary leader, his persona, knowledge, experience, wisdom and articulation skills endear him to many and he continues to be a source of encouragement and inspiration to all. Additionally, he guides the corporate world on subjects of governance and ethics, and is truly an enabler of excellence.

❑

Chapter 4

A Person, Persona, Personality and Professional Par Excellence

– Sushil Kumar
Ex-secretary to GOI

When Mr. M. Damodaran, as a young teenager, suddenly decided to quit the engineering degree course mid-way at the premier institute of IIT (Madras - as it was then known as), one can only guess that, he must have had some strange premonition that mastery in making machines, manufacturing materials and earning a huge salary could not have been his calling. It seems that even an assured promising career prospect, cushioned with cool comforts of an air conditioned chateau, complemented with countless credit cards, ceaseless cash flows wasn't going to be his calling. Possibly, he had a moment of reckoning, when it dawned upon him that dealing with matters and affairs of mankind motivated him more than the mere comforts of a cushy corporate life and a corner office of the CEO.

Accepting Challenges

One is sure that his family would have felt bewildered, beyond belief, to discover their ward's self-assured steps into the senior years. They knew he was a precocious child when he told them about his one on one confident conversation with India's Prime Minister Pt. Jawahar Lal Nehru during his visit to school. They must have been taken aback on seeing the early signs of their teenaged son, seeking to straightaway jump to swim against the surging currents of life. Perhaps, his passion for playing the game of chess, and combating the contours of complex crossword puzzles (of Statesman vintage), had bred in him an irrepressible feeling of experiencing the incomparable thrill of adrenalin rush, while conquering tough challenges, on a continuous basis especially when odds are stacked against oneself. This leitmotif seems to have defined the entire course of his career. It has also defined the recurring patterns in his personality of preferring to pick up challenges throughout the path of professional progression. And despite his advancing years, this leitmotif continues to dominate his decisions even to this day. In other words, it would be apt to say that never expect the expected from the man. He likes to spring surprises on others including oneself.

If one were to describe in a word as to what encapsulates the life, living, love and times of Mr. Damodaran, only one word immediately comes to mind, and that is 'leader'. In this assessment, there is unanimity of opinion amongst his peers and others. Personally, I would prefer to qualify that description by using the epithet of 'natural born leader' as it fully fits his person and personality.

IAS Provided Wings/ Desired Space

He also was bang on target when he instinctively chose the career path of being an IAS officer; it alone could fulfil his aspiration of being in the leadership role, starting from the first post of a sub- divisional magistrate and culminating in the Secretary/ Chief Secretary. IAS continues to be the leadership service till this day. This is borne out by the fact that over a million apply every year and over half million actually take the preliminary examinations. Add to the fact that top private sector corporate honchos continue to crave and choose to join the government at equivalent levels through lateral intake.

A Natural Leader

The above description of a natural born leader may be at variance with the generally accepted maxim on leadership penned by Vince Lombardi- stating that the leaders aren't born but are made through hard work. One feels that Mr. Damodaran is one rare individual who combines the traits of being a natural born leader with the rigours of hard work in somewhat equal measure. He has proven himself, time and again, in situations where leadership traits mattered more than hard work and equally in those where inverse calculations counted and were called out.

Mr. Damodaran loves being continuously challenged and invariably ends up being the first one to step forward, especially when few choose to take up the cudgels for an unequal contest. More than someone casting a challenge, he himself likes being tested by tough assignments especially when he is sent to set the broken house and put things in order. This was best exemplified when he was sent to restore the faith of the small investors, securities and stock markets, when the UTI was on the brink of collapse. The parliament's functioning was stalled daily, and the head of India's finance minister was on the block. The job of nursing a failing national institution back to health, while all its parameters were heading southwards, was definitely not for the taking by the faint hearted. It may be recalled that the collapse of US-64, of UTI in 2001 engineered a national level debate on banishing insider trading- a bane afflicting public financial institutions since India's independence. In that hour of national crisis looming over India's financial sector, Mr. Damodaran was promptly sent on a rescue mission to salvage, strengthen and sustain the broken system; and save a fully 'stocked' sinking ship going off the course busting the bourses on the course. Most people would have thought twice before accepting such a testy assignment where waters were muddied by allegations of political manipulation, corporate greed and massive misgovernance. Despite being a total novice in the big business world of Bombay, no one opposed or commented on his selection to head the mission. It is to his credit that the govt. didn't think as to how a bureaucrat from a small cadre like Tripura could be considered to take up the challenge, especially when the State's association with the description of a stock exchange, is comparable to an Icelander coming over to thaw in the Thar desert.

Let me state how I failed to find a single stockbroker while trying to purchase UTI's Master Equity Plan 92 at Agartala. I eventually purchased MEP 92, from Delhi, for ten thousand Rupees. It is a different story that my fate also somehow got linked with the Harshad Mehta securities scam unfolding in 1992 and what eventually happened to UTI/ US- 64 in 2002. Finally, UTI returned the same amount of initial investment after keeping the amount for ten long years. One regretted dreaming to derive the spoils of corporate gains, after a decade of India's liberalization, launched in 1991. Ten thousand seems a small amount today but was quite a handful when one's total salary was four thousand rupees.

Not only did Mr. Damodaran come out with flying colours by restoring public faith in the functioning of a national level institution like the Unit Trust of India, he also designed a detailed plan for regulating mutual funds operations to obtain transparency and accountability. A system of determining Net Asset Value of stocks stocked with the UTI was also initiated. He also built synergies between the UTI and the SEBI and it eventually led to his transition as head of the SEBI. It was during his time that the SEBI took final steps in building an end to end regulatory architecture based on the latest information and communication technologies. When teaching as visiting professor at IMT,

Ghaziabad, ten years ago, one learnt that India's regulatory regime governing stock markets is considered even better than that of the US.

It seems that while working as the Joint Secretary in the Department of Banking, Govt. of India, Mr. Damodaran had learnt the lessons well during handling the collateral damage to the system, that was caused by the securities scam, perpetrated by Harshad Mehta. His experience combined with direct hands-on dealing with the US-64 crisis enabled him to design an ecosystem that has broadly stood the test of time. It may seem that one is too effusive in heaping praise on a member of one's ilk. To put this beyond an expression of a biased person's adulation, let me quote what The Economic Times dated 27th October 2007 wrote. "For Damodaran, steering SEBI has been yet another challenge, after administering UTI and subsequently IDBI, two institutions that were facing a grave crisis." One cannot miss the heading which stated, "Policy Change Agent M Damodaran: Turnaround specialist, demolition man." This aptly describes his personality and character.

Well Connected with people at the Bottom of Social Segment

After I Joined the State government as a probationer in the year 1988, the name of Mr. Damodaran, despite his absence, was invoked by everyone - as being the first IAS officer in the cadre. Of course, the public service orientation of Tripura government and serving under the legendary Chief Minister, Mr. Nripen Chakraborty and the Chief Secretary, Mr. Sankaran (both had only two sets of clothes) had instilled a caring attitude towards a man of modest means in Shri Damodaran. Added to this, Mr. Damodaran 's personal handling of the humanitarian crisis of people's displacement during Bangladesh's war and the migration of Chakmas cemented the compassionate component in his choices/decisions during the later part of his official journey. One guesses that dealing with poverty, and providing provisions for the underprivileged people bred in him the propensity to apply the 'talisman' test prescribed by Gandhiji. Despite being at the top, he is God gifted with the ability to seamlessly connect with people at the bottom end of the social segment. Perhaps, this explains why Mr. Damodaran is more popular with the subordinate staff, irrespective of the places and postings in his illustrious career.

Mr. Damodaran began his journey as a civil servant from Tripura, in the seventies, dealing mostly with poverty alleviation projects and ended up as the head of the national regulatory body, dealing with the matters of companies and corporate governance. Nothing can be as contrasting as him taking the Fokker Friendship plane in 1972, with chicken coops at the back, to flying first class to the farthest corners of the world, to advise on complex matters of corporate governance, three decades later. Even though he has slowed down on his commitments, he still is on the board of Indigo- India's premier airline, that is flying high and continues to climb higher in the skies and conquer all competition especially when the other airlines are either coming to a grinding halt or are grounded. No wonder, the owners don't want him to fly away into retirement with all the concentrated corporate wisdom kept to himself.

Rare Category of Civil Servant

Coming from rather humble beginnings, it is the boon of the Civil Service that I have had the fortune of meeting several bureaucrats who lived with the tag of being the 'first' in certain matters. Mr. Damodaran was the first IAS officer of Tripura segment (of the then joint Manipur Tripura cadre) and was the first and youngest when he became the Chief Secretary of a State Govt. merely after twenty years of service. Another officer was Mr.

G. S. Sial who belonged to the first batch of the IAS when India became independent in 1947. I also had the fortune of meeting Shri Kamat, ICS, who was one of the eight Secretaries to the Govt. of India when India became independent. All these three officers are really from another world - civil services should be very proud of.

Always Accessible to Subordinates

During the probationary period, I had made a documentary on the IAS Academy which was appreciated by the then director Shri B.N. Yugandhar. At that time only Doordarshan existed, and I wanted it to be telecast there. On learning that Shri Damodaran was posted in Delhi, in Doordarshan, I hesitantly went to meet him. As is usual in the corridors of power in Delhi, his personal staff told me that he was in a meeting. Nevertheless, they sent in the slip and asked me to wait. To my surprise, I was called in within seconds of the slip being sneaked in. Upon entering, he welcomed me with a smile, asked me to sit and stalled the meeting midway. This was in total contrast to some officers, with just a couple of years seniority, who treat the probationers almost like subordinate staff. His assuring and encouraging welcoming tone put me at ease. He listened to my wish and immediately spoke to someone on intercom and called one staff and directed me to be taken to that room. He asked me to keep him apprised of further developments. The concerned official asked me to show the film which was in the custody of the Academy. I stated that I would send the film after going back to State. I returned to Tripura and couldn't send the film due to the fact that from that interior town of Kailshahar, it was easier to visit Bangladesh than to send/dispatch the film. Those were still the days of the Indian Post Office playing around with Postcards, Inland letters and the Aerogram and sending a magnetic tape would have been a tough task. I gave up the efforts to telecast the film on Doordarshan as one lived really 'Door' from Delhi and despite the doors of Doordarshan having been opened for me, darshaana of the film on Doordarshan remained a distant dream (door ka darshan). However, I couldn't ever forget the encouragement from an officer (Mr Damodaran) who didn't know me at all and when I went to meet him without any reference or recommendation (as is usual in our service); had yet welcomingly opened his door to meet a probationer sans any preconceived perceptions. This trait of not being dismissive of subordinate staff has contributed to his immense acceptance within the civil services.

As is well known, the government system is notorious for not only functioning at a snail's speed but also through hierarchical levels, with each level operating almost as an independent system. Sometimes, one is inclined to conclude that the Indian system may be mimicking the multitudinous levels and layers of the Indian caste system with each level operating as an endogamous group. In contrast, the private sector operates on relatively flatter hierarchies, with far fewer levels to foster efficiency and effectiveness. Mr. Damodaran realized that for him to be an effective and efficient manager, the channels of communication and access need to be calibrated as per calculations of immediate tasks and long term goals. That is a tough job as the ground rules tend to vary from situations to positions. It is to his credit that he has that uncanny ability to understand and unravel what action is required in a particular situation. For example, during the domineering days of the then Chief Election Commissioner, Shri T.N. Seshan, when postponement of an election process could be ordered on a trivial ground of slight delay in providing of a vehicle to an election observer, Mr. Damodaran, as the Chief Secretary, chose to allow direct access to the protocol officers so that things are monitored on a minute to minute basis. Now, that can give the impression of being a micromanager but, as we all know, no risks could be taken when Mr. Seshan was the CEC.

Forget the C.S. even the C.Ms were concerned by the famous temper and tantrums of the then CEC.

This quality to communicate, sometimes simultaneously, across all levels in a hierarchical system, if the situation so sought, is distinct and has defined his style of leadership. For that reason, his information has infinite inlets and gets updated in real time. This necessitates building a much larger team beyond his immediate level and this strategy has helped him to harness the energy of an entire system cumulatively. It has helped him drive the organisations and individuals to transcend limitations of government systems to scale stupendous heights.

An Example in Efficient Corporate Governance

As stated, his open access or 'open source' style of functioning has helped in communication of the goals clearly, across all levels, especially in the government spawned systems, spread in several layers. Otherwise, the gnawing gap in communication of goals, and expectations from each level, can adversely affect the results, especially in situations where one is sent, and is in unfamiliar territory, to do the fire fighting and show results. This has led to his belonging to a class of bureaucrats, who can visualize and stimulate simultaneity of action of all levels. This way he can keep a constant watch on the big picture as well as on the small picture and calibrate course corrective actions as per the evolving situation. To put in other words, the dynamism of Mr. Damodaran's leadership style stems from understanding that all situations are dynamic and there is no one straightjacketed solution to suit or solve all situations. It is for these reasons, it seems that he has found his final calling in setting up a think tank (Excellence Enablers) for preparing future leaders for the country, especially in corporate governance. He continues to be a visiting professor for several national and international academic and other institutions.

Unflappable and Unflustered Nature

One is yet to see him raise his tone or show temper while dealing with tough problems or persons. He has not allowed his character-defining trait of decency to drop under even in the most demanding situations. He extends cordiality and courtesy to all who come in contact with him, irrespective of whether they are still in service or not. This has allowed even people, who disagree with him, to remain in touch for long periods of time. People say that a man's visage displays his inner emotions, but Mr. Damodaran can mask his feelings rather well and though he hasn't played poker, playing chess must have taught him that one shouldn't wear the emotions on one's sleeve.

However, the most unique quality that separates him from his peers, especially in tough testy situations is that familiar natural smile that rarely disappears from his face, and even if it does on rare occasions, it rarely ends up in a frown. In such rare situations, at most, he orders a cup of tea and gulps down the discomfort and tasteless Tripura tea and tries diverting deliberations to some other issue. For me he still remains the only person in service who never shouted at anyone or threw the files or the person out of office - a trait that is touted as a trademark of a tough officer.

He has been bestowed with a great sense of humour and this gift is complemented with having a perfect sense of timing while narrating tales. He has a great gift of lightening the moods of everyone in the room. I still remember the times when the entire Tripura police was on strike, but he hardly displayed any strain when one attended the review meeting.

Full of Wit and Wisdom

He also combines a unique and a rare mix of having enormous experience (*anubhuti*), with power of expression (*abhivyakti*) in equal measure. Due to this, give him any situation and context, however serious, and trust him to come out with one liners and wisecracks, laced with wit and wisdom. However, to fully partake that part of his personality, one has to have an understanding and love of the English language. For that reason, sometimes in Tripura, his humorous take was taken seriously, inviting a rather negative response. But in the megapolises of Mumbai, Delhi and Manhattan, his self-deprecating and understated humour continues to be lapped up and receive adulation.

In acknowledgement of his talent of being a class communicator, he continues to receive invitations from national/international academia, policy think tanks, corporate world and others. Inspired, one also learnt to understand and use the nuances of spoken and written language over a period of time. He inspired several people to learn how to say the same thing/s differently by using different word/s to disguise distinct differences. His recounting of experiences, in drafting replies to parliament questions, regaled us all; this taught us how to balance the intricacies of being correct and avoiding causing controversies, lest one was repatriated back to the cadre on the same day. Working with him helped me to become a columnist for sports, films and cultural affairs, over a period of time.

As a natural leader with immense intuitive powers, he instinctively ends up selecting the right team including individual/s and bestows it with full authority and then backs them up to the hilt - sometimes to the extent of even displeasing the political executive. I know of a case when the govt. advised in writing to transfer the officer, not once but thrice, but he persisted to back the officer, knowing well that when the goal would be achieved, the govt. would appreciate the outcome. However, the govt. is not always as interested in getting the goals achieved as it is to assert the supremacy of the political executive, often just to prove a point.

Take Full Responsibility Even for Subordinates

He leads from the front and takes full responsibility for the actions of his subordinates – a quality that has become rarer as one has progressed in the civil services over the last four decades. This is not an empty statement; but one borne out by the fact that he supported several officers, refused to retreat and baulked at leaving them stranded mid-way. The political executives perceived this as defiance and it led to serious differences during his posting as the Chief Secretary. It did damage his career at some point, but he refused to sack the officer/s as sacrificial goat/s especially when asked to get the same job done initially. One also learnt from him that whatever be the provocation, one shouldn't bite the bait immediately, but respond and play the game at a time and place of one's choosing. One has tried to emulate this in one's career but failed as perception of a perfect timing is an art not bestowed on all and sundry.(In contrast most of the officers blindly follow the orders of political bosses as long as it does not hurt them or affect them)

Forgive and Forget is One of the Essence of His Character

It now seems clear that in the true tradition of being a civil servant transcending considerations of caste, region and religion, Mr. Damodaran's team, irrespective of the organization, has always reflected the diversity of India. This characteristic was evident decades before diversity became the buzzword in this century. Due to this, he commands a lifelong loyalty amongst most of his team members. If someone chose to walk away, no vengeful response was ever engineered subsequently; because he felt wasting one's energy in negative efforts affected the doer first and the other much later. This special quality has kept Mr. Damodaran in good health. He has an infinite capacity to forgive and forget. He is known to de-stress by diverting his attention in relishing the gourmet food. He loves delicacies of every kind and am sure he has tasted the best cuisines of the world. It has possibly emanated from his being born in Kerala, studying in Madras (then) and Delhi, serving in north eastern India, working and living in Delhi and Mumbai and straddling the corridors of the corporate world across the globe.

The tale of Mr. Damodaran harnessing the raw energy of a young officer is legendary. On receipt of reports of serious wrongdoings within a department, he posted a young officer, full of idealism and enthusiasm, to change things. When the officer went full force to change things, he also treaded on some familiar interests and the government wanted his immediate replacement. As a leader, he didn't want to leave a young officer crestfallen on being changed and wanted to prevent him from being a cynic in his career. He dilly-dallied issuing the transfer order for a while and despite the mounting political heat, Mr. Damodaran didn't let the young man down. When the young man realized the full picture, it was inevitable that he would remain his lifelong protégé. In this case, one must note that the Departmental Minister from the coalition was so supportive that he called a press conference to back the official. It is indeed rare that a Departmental Minister supports the official so openly to the peril of his political pursuits. It is a different matter that his political career also plummeted post his picking the public policy over political priorities.

Mr. Damodaran often casts aside the cool confines of the comfort zone and happily accepts new challenges. He has been very brave in openly encouraging the implementation of new ideas and promoting /encouraging experimental efforts initiated by the young officers. For example, he gave full support to the pioneering ideas of a young officer to invite national level bodies, like the National Dairy Development Board and the Venkateshwara Hatcheries to help a small state like Tripura. He encouraged the officer to go and directly talk to the legendary leaders like Mr. V. Kurien and Dr. B.V. Rao who had revolutionized the Indian way of doing business. Actually, both these famous figures were taken aback that a small state like Tripura was approaching them for partnerships. Though it was neither economically viable nor technically feasible for them to come to Tripura, they still decided to help Tripura in the early nineties, when the celebrated signing of MoUs had not hit the states big time. Mr. Damodaran was aware that these were difficult endeavours and likely to falter but he still backed up the officer. He didn't want to discourage a young officer from trying out the big ideas in a small state. Much after Mr. Damodaran left Tripura, the State Government remembered his pioneering efforts in introducing the supply of day old ducklings at one rupee and for linking Tripura with the national poultry development program. As they say, in 1993, this small step was a giant leap in linking the poultry sector with the national supply chain. Small States, especially in the north east, have innumerable bottlenecks, infrastructural and communicational, and pose challenges to build and buttress the initial successes. Public memory is proverbially short, specially of political participants, but few can deny the first steps undertaken when Mr. Damodaran was in charge.

The success achieved by Mr. Damodaran is all the more credible as it was achieved in a small State. Ask those who have worked in the North Eastern States, Himachal Pradesh and Haryana, where no issue is too small and big issues are blown to be bigger than they actually are. Working in these States requires grit, application, tenacity and determination to grind through the endless tests. These trials and tribulations make the Tripura officers tenacious and when the chance comes to work in the big States or at the national level, one has the experience of learning, derived from working and looking at both the big and the small pictures. This must have contributed to the super success of Shri Damodaran and of others at the national and international levels.

Management Skills Par Excellence

His greatest characteristic is that unlike all the top achievers in most fields, he never asks for new person/s or for changing members of the old team. He has always worked with the tools given to him; he understands that neither is there a perfect person to do the job nor is there a perfect solution. All situations defy permanent, or one time solutions and most attempts are work in progress. Take the examples of LIC, SEBI, IDBI and innumerable intractable issues of/in the State Government. Even these institutions haven't found the final solutions for everything. Knowing this, he intuitively assesses the potential and talent of each member and then assigns them the matching tasks. He loves proving the pundits wrong and often deliberately chooses an underdog or the discarded one to do and deliver. When such persons are entrusted with the responsibility they didn't anticipate, they work tirelessly to not let down the trust and responsibility bestowed on them.

I have never seen him show his authority to the people working under him. Displaying the trait of a true warrior,he tests the ground and contests the issues with the people in positions of power, especially the ones above him. This shows his belief in certain core convictions and the will to wage a battle for the principles which cannot be compromised lest they jeopardise the institutions and systemic integrity.

One must remember that Tripura hardly had any institutional existence, related to private banking or insurance, where an officer could cut teeth to gain any semblance of experience in such matters. It is to his credit that unlike a recent appointment to the post of Governor of Reserve Bank of India, no one asked about his qualification or experience while giving responsibilities of national level institutions like the UTI, SEBI, IDBI etc. Everyone just thought that he was the right fit for the job, quite like his own self- belief that he could handle any tough assignment. Not only did he successfully scale the summits of these rather intimidating peaks, but he still continues to reinvent himself in the fields of corporate governance and leadership. Today, he is considered as the leading guru in the domain of corporate governance and grooming of future leaders in corporate excellence.

While handling tough assignments of different hues, like all successful leaders, he keeps his approach rather simple. This trait is bestowed only on a select few, who can identify the core issue and stay clear of the clutter, continuing taking concerted action on combating the contentious issues contained therein. This seems simple but requires a mind typical of a Zen master having the ability to convert complex matters into simple ones.

Today, his eminent status as a corporate governance guru is universally acknowledged. He is a Director on the Board of India's premier airline - Indigo. His career, which began in the seventies, continues to soar in the skies, in his mid-seventies too. His penchant for pursuing new career challenges is equally matched by the Indigo's potential to scale newer heights. It was inevitable that, with him at the helm, the airline is soaring to greater heights every day, both nationally and internationally. Seeing that the sky and space is limitless, Mr. Damodaran has spread his wings fully to soar for some more time and have an aerial view of issues of corporate governance. His vast experience and a bird's eye view of corporate functioning enables him to render expert advice to both the old and the new of the corporate world. In other words, his words count and advice matters in issues of the corporate world.

An Excellent Orator and A Great Story Teller

He is a great teacher, in the sense that he is an enabler and empowers people to imagine and push the limits to the possible and live up to their dreams. I, for one, was privileged to be enabled by him and it has been a matter of privilege to be called his protégé.

There never was and never can be a dull moment when we all sit down with Mr. Damodaran. He is bestowed with an elephantine memory, matched with a talent, to nuance and narrate a tale that touches. I hope to seek his time to compile all the tales of Tripura one day. In his memory bank, there are a million tales and it would be such a loss if that treasure is not preserved.

His talent for telling timeless anecdotes is matchless. It is not for nothing that his wife, children, colleagues and corporate dote on him when he opens his memory bank of anecdotes. My guess is that this talent or '*sanskaar*' got passed on to his kids- one is a leading lawyer of international repute and the other was a poet prodigy once and is now an international expert with mastery in that other language - the computer language.

Sadly, my arrival at Delhi on deputation coincided with his changing location to Mumbai. Intense involvement in family matters, especially in raising a disabled kid, caused gaps in social interaction for nearly two decades and the loss is entirely mine. It is only since the last few years that the connection has been restored, and one feels that he had never been far away from us.

I often wonder why people haven't used the abbreviation of MD in lieu of his name (M. Damodaran.) Perhaps, he wasn't supposed to be an MD (remember he left the IIT) but was destined to deal with matters of MDs and CMDs and hence destiny desisted from attaching that epithet to his name.

I shall await the day one can read his autobiography. I suggest that he writes one. One doesn't want that the concerted words of wisdom on administration – private or public - is not accessible to the younger generation. I draw his attention to his effusive admiration of Shri B.K. Nehru, Governor of Tripura and his memoirs titled 'Nice Guys Finish Second'; and suggest that he should also pen his memoirs for several reasons.

❑

Chapter 5

Mr M Damodaran as I know Him

– **VK Bahuguna**
Retd. Indian Forest Service Officer

Civil services are one of the best platforms to serve the country as civil servants bring happiness to the people through their dedication, hard work and by solving people's problems without fear and favours. Civil servants in a democratic country have to work in a milieu surrounded by the politicians and are responsible for advising them to implement the policies of the government directed at welfare of the masses. The tiny state of Tripura was one of the few fairly well administered states in the country, at least till civil servants like me were in the state. The state has also produced top class politicians, administrators, policy planners and professionals. I have always wanted to join the Indian Forest Service (IFS) and Tripura being a forested state with 60 % area under forest cover and a sizable Tribal population of 30 % provided me a great opportunity to work for the state.

Charismatic Leader With Extraordinary Skills

In my 37 years of professional career in the government at the centre and in the state, one of the fine innovative administrators with charming personality, grace with human face, someone I admire the most, is none other than Mr M Damodaran who was our senior colleague, but always behaved as friend, philosopher and guide to junior officers of all services. Mr Damodaran exudes all traits of a charismatic leader with extraordinary skills of communication that is colourful, imaginative yet carried out in a straightforward manner with commitment to the rule book and avowed policies of the government. He would encourage, guide and support the young officers so that they would feel motivated and be proud of the profession. He would go to any length to protect the officers from undesirable political interference and also from the vitiated internal problems faced due to upright officers in their domain.

Unflinching Support to Subordinates

My acquaintance with Mr Damodaran increased after I returned to Tripura when I sought premature repatriation in June 1993 from the Indian Institute of Forest Management (IIFM), Bhopal in 1993, where I was working as Professor and Coordinator of a Government of India's Centre for Social Forestry. It was Mr Damodaran who prompted me to return to the state and as the Chief Secretary, he posted me as the Conservator of Forests, Northern Circle Kumarghat and Ex-officio Deputy Chief Wildlife Warden in August 1993. Of the two Forest Circles Northern Circle was the biggest and the forest administration was in turmoil because the state was rocked by a massive timber scandal in 'Jampui hill' and also by insurgency. When I was at IIFM I received a letter in 1992 from veteran Communist leader and former Chief Minister and the then leader of opposition Nripen Chakraborty (whom I knew since my days as DFO Teliamura under which his Pramod Nagar Constituency falls) about the timber scandal and he requested me to raise this issue. As luck would have it, as soon as I joined, I was asked to conduct an inquiry on the 'Jampui' timber scandal with the assistance of one Assistant Conservator of Forests. The environment in the department was made hostile because the senior most officer of the department wanted the inquiry to be done in a manner which would do no justice as some of his cronies were behind protecting the culprits. It was the unflinching support of Mr Damodaran as Chief Secretary in-charge of Forest Department that in spite of insurmountable obstacles, I was able to complete the inquiry and based on the report of inquiry, a senior officer of forest department was charge sheeted. I had easy access to him any time even when he was busy in the meetings and it shows the nature and quality of a great leader of men and material.

Problem Solving Leader

I would like to narrate two episodes which I remember and believe will reflect on the quality of his perception and his way to lead and deal with junior officers who are not directly under him. In May 1994 while working as Conservator of Forests, I was invited by the Society for Wasteland Development in Delhi to attend and Chair a session on a National Seminar on Joint Forest Management (JFM) at Shillong. The JFM was a new initiative in the forest departments as per the National Forest Policy of 1988. At the IIFM, I had initiated efforts to spread the success of this programme across the states at the national level. So they requested me to share my experience. I had written to the Principal Chief Conservator of Forests, Tripura requesting permission for attending the seminar at Shillong as it would be a good opportunity to share with the participants what Tripura was doing and also learn from the other states. The regular PCCF was on leave and another CCF was in charge. This officer had an ego issue with me and had always been jealous of me though I had always been respectful to him. As the date of seminar was nearing, I phoned him around 20th May 1994, seeking permission but he point blank refused permission and banged his phone down. So I immediately informed the organizers about my inability to attend the seminar at Shillong. Just three days before the seminar I got a phone call again that since I was slated to Chair a session they were requesting me to apply for casual leave and attend and promised to pay the taxi charges from my place of posting to Shillong and back. I then contacted the office of the Chief Secretary and requested Mr Damodaran's staff to connect me to him. After five minutes I got a call from the Chief Secretary's office and I spoke to Mr Damodaran and briefed him about the Shillong seminar and the proposal of the organizers to pay the cost of travel for attending the seminar. I also informed him about the senior officer in charge not agreeing to my request to participate and refusing to allow even casual leave. After carefully listening and considering the importance of the event, Mr Damodaran asked me to write the casual leave application addressed to the Chief Secretary and forward it through the PCCF office and leave the station to attend the seminar. I did the same and attended the seminar at Shillong. In any case the powers to sanction casual leave for going outside the state rested with the government. This reflects the attitude of empathy while treating the officers with respect and excellent display of social and leadership skills and ability to amicably settle the issues.

I would like to narrate another instance of his professional commitment as an astute administrator. This is regarding his taking a very professionally and administratively tough yet correct stand as Secretary in-charge of the forest department on the state government's '*suo motto*' attempts to withdraw a notification of seventies declaring 2000 hectares of government land as Protected Forests. He warned the political leadership and the Chief Minister of violation of the Forest Conservation Act (FC Act) 1980. But after he left, the next incumbent Secretary advised the government and the notification was withdrawn. So long he was in Tripura, it did not happen and he was proved right even after the Protected Forests were de-notified yet the state government could not use this land as they wished and the land had to be classified as Unclassed Forests and continued to invite the provisions of FC Act 1980. He was one of the best Chief Secretaries of Tripura and people fondly remember him for his outstanding behaviour and skills.

After leaving Tripura, Mr Damodaran turned around many institutions of the Government of India and will always be remembered for his contributions. After his superannuation he is a much sought after expert in stock market and financial matters. He is a brilliant speaker as well and I observed this quality when I as Director-General of Indian Council of Forestry Research and Education (ICFRE) and Chancellor of Forest Research Institute—a Deemed University had invited him to address the scientists and students in 1992. His lecture was very well appreciated and rated very highly by the audience, especially by the students. I firmly believe that civil servants of Mr Damodaran's calibre are an invaluable asset for the nation.

❑

Chapter 6

Efficiently Managing Political Leadership

– Rajeshwar Rao
Retd IAS

I joined the IAS in the year 1988 and was allotted the Tripura state of Manipur - Tripura cadre. Being from the Southern State of Andhra Pradesh, the state of Tripura with its different social and administrative culture, was challenging and unique. Tripura is one of very few States in the country where IAS is truly the "Civil servant " and it enables officers to imbibe the ethos of a "service first" approach. It was initially an eye opener but soon became a joyful experience as I always wanted to be in the service, to serve the community especially the weaker sections of the society. Tripura had a large population of tribals (about 30 %) and provided the opportunity to understand them closely, appreciate their culture and belief and work for their welfare and overall development.

Caring and Warm Attitude

When I first met Mr Damodaran, in mid-1989, he was a senior civil servant of Tripura cadre and I was impressed by his caring and warm attitude towards the junior officers and especially towards me. Even though I was one of the junior-most officers, yet he treated me with respect and identified my inner strengths. This worked as a stimulant and motivated me to perform optimally and also experiment/take risks, for the welfare of the people, as there was always someone to look up to and take guidance and support from. During the long journey of 34 years, and even after superannuation, he continues to be a pillar of support and strength, with the same warmth and caring relationship.

When he became the chief secretary, he ensured that a probationer was received by the protocol officer at the airport, given the posting letter/order (as assistant collector), allotted suitable accommodation and the other logistic requirements were also taken care of. Before this, when the young recruit (IAS) would come to join the state, he would have to get a private taxi to reach the circuit house(generally a shared one), wait for allotment of room in circuit house and pursue to get his/her posting orders. Earlier when a young officer had to visit the secretariat, he had to either walk down (a distance of 3-4 Km) or take a public bus or private three wheeler/taxi. Seniors generally especially from the State services were not very supportive of the young direct recruit officers during the period before Mr Damodaran became the Chief Secretary. As he must have undergone/faced similar issues when he had first joined the State, he ensured that all the new / young officers are looked after and made to feel proud of belonging to the State. This action of his resulted in motivating the young officers so as to enable them to perform more efficiently and diligently. He would personally meet the young officers and listen to their issues / suggestions to improve the functioning of the State administration. It was a very rare gesture for a senior civil servant to show concern for the young one.

Efficiently Managing Contradiction

Mr Damodaran's career is truly remarkable and exemplary in many aspects. Despite being the youngest civil servant to ever hold the position of Chief Secretary, the administrative head of the state, he worked very successfully with divergent political philosophies as head of administration. His skill to manage contradiction efficiently is very unique (managing political aspiration without compromising on rules and regulations). Mr Damodaran managed to navigate the complex political and administrative challenges with incredible skill and grace. He remained committed to his principles and his mission to serve the people of the state, and continued to lead the administration with dedication and determination. He used to provide guidance to the Chief Minister fearlessly (despite the opposition from the other members of the Council of Ministers - majority being non-tribal) and protected junior civil servants, so that they could perform optimally to the best of their abilities. He ensured a free and fair election – no repoll was done in any constituency, despite the chequered history of Tripura elections with large incidents of violence, unacceptable practices etc. His support to the field level functionaries ensured that administration maintained neutrality in every action related to the performance and conduct of the election.

Generally there is some rift between the state civil service and the IAS and managing the aspirations of both the groups (both have different associations) is always a challenge. Efficient handling of the diverse group aspirations is a unique skill of Mr Damodaran. Once he was invited to the annual general meeting of the state civil services and asked to address the audience. His speech was very much appreciated by all the state officers present there.

"TCS officers are like Ambassador cars. They never ditch their passengers mid-way. Whatever malfunction may occur in their operating system, Ambassador cars somehow safely take their passengers to their destination. Like Ambassador cars, TCS officers might whimper for all the deficiencies they suffer from but never faltered in delivering goods to the people."

He paused for a while, glanced at the spellbound faces of his officers and resumed.

"IAS officers are like new-age Maruti cars. They run on new technology unknown to the abundantly available mechanics. If they encounter even a very insignificant mechanical or electrical glitch, the Maruti cars will not move an inch. TCS officers build the foundations, and the IAS officers build buildings on such foundations."

Most of the state service officers were great fans of Mr Damodaran as he never underestimated their contribution in managing the affairs of the state administration.

Promote Innovation and New Initiatives

Thanks to his leadership, the Tripura state administration was able to overcome many of its most pressing challenges and make considerable progress in a wide range of areas, particularly socio-economic development of tribals, *chakma* refugee rehabilitation, land alienation issues, development of entrepreneurs from socially deprived classes, promoting women leadership, development of rubber and tea plantation, *prashasanik shibirs* (administrative camps) - taking administration to the doorsteps of people and many other unique developmental initiatives. His ability to manage complex issues, build consensus, and inspire his colleagues and subordinates was truly remarkable, and is a testament to his extraordinary skill and character. His unflinching support and encouragement to his colleagues is an inspiration to all who know him. I feel fortunate to have had the opportunity to work very closely with him as I was the secretary to the Chief Minister, when he was the chief secretary in the State.

Extending Care and Support Even for Personal Problems

I will narrate an example of Mr Damodaran's personal care, generosity and leadership. One incident that particularly stands out in my mind is when I needed to urgently visit my ailing mother in Hyderabad. I was unsure as to how to make the trip, given the urgency of the situation, but Mr Damodaran immediately volunteered to help and arranged everything for me. Thanks to his efforts, I was able to visit my mother in time, which brought her great relief and comfort. He is an example for others in civil services in providing support to colleagues when they have any personal problem. One can always freely approach him without hesitation whenever there is any help or support required, even for personal matters. He has been a "Fatherly" figure for all those who worked with him.

Multi-Tasking Skills

Mr Damodaran is truly a master of multitasking. I have seen him juggle numerous tasks with ease, never once losing his cool or his focus. He has a remarkable ability to engage with people, read official notes, issue instructions to his personal secretary and manage other tasks simultaneously. It is truly awe-inspiring to watch him in action.It is not just his multitasking skills that are impressive, but his dictation skills are utterly amazing too. He speaks clearly and concisely, with a command over the language that is exceptional. His instructions are always lucid and easy to understand, which makes it simple to follow his lead/ direction. He has a proficiency in vocabulary, grammar and syntax that is second to none. When he speaks, he commands attention and his words carry weight and authority with no confusion or dilemma in decision making.

I feel fortunate to have worked with such an exceptional leader and civil servant. His multitasking abilities, dictation skills, and command of the English language are just a few of the many qualities that make him such a remarkable person. Overall, his career is a testament to his resilience, his leadership skills, and his unwavering commitment to serving the people of the state. His legacy will be remembered for years to come and his contributions to the civil service and the community are truly exceptional and will be remembered for long.

When he joined the State in 1971, he was the first officer to be allotted after Tripura was separated from the Union Territory cadre. The conditions were difficult, especially on the personal front. He was once called by the District magistrate in the early morning hours and asked to visit a place where the Tribals were refusing to hand over the bodies of the two non -tribals whom they had killed. A large number of tribals had gathered at a place with arms and were very angry with the administration. It was becoming a major tribal - non tribal conflict. Mr Damodaran visited the place with a few police constables. After reaching the place of incidence, he went and met the people without taking the police with him (the police team was asked to stay at the nearby location). Initially the tribals were very hostile but he could persuade them to hand over the bodies of the non-tribals and assured them due justice would be done to their grievances. He was called by the chief secretary on the next day and asked to write down the entire process of handling the sensitive situation. Later the chief secretary circulated the same process as SOP(Standard operating process) to all the field officers in a meeting. His handling of the difficult / crisis situation became a model for other field functionaries in the State.

Never Afraid to Speak the Truth—Fearlessness

One of the most remarkable things about Mr Damodaran was his fearlessness in guiding the Chief Minister of the state. He was never afraid to speak the truth and offer his honest opinion on matters of public policy and administration. His unwavering commitment to doing what was right for the people of the state was truly inspiring and he earned the respect and admiration of his colleagues and subordinates alike.

It was not just the Chief Minister that the senior civil servant protected and guided, he was also deeply committed to protecting junior civil servants and ensuring that they were provided the support and guidance as required to perform their duties to the best of their ability. He knew that the success of the state administration depended on the collective efforts of all its members, and he worked tirelessly to create an environment where everyone could thrive and contribute their best. Thanks to his leadership and guidance, countless civil servants were able to grow and develop in their careers. His commitment to public service and his unwavering dedication to doing what was right for the people of the state will be remembered for years to come.

Simple Living and Ability to Appreciate Others Point of View

Mr Damodaran had a unique personality and style of functioning that set him apart from his colleagues. He had a simple routine, consisting of a standard meal every day of two deeply fried fish pieces, Begun Bhaja (deep fried Brinjal) and he would often have late lunch. He was always focused and attentive when it came to his official duties. His informal way of meeting colleagues was inspiring to everyone in the administration. His ability to listen to others point of view, appreciate and then suggest appropriate steps/ approach without hurting or undermining the others, especially the juniors, is a rare quality amongst the civil servants. If he needed to meet with a visiting official urgently, he would not hesitate to call them in for a meeting, even if it were outside of normal working hours. He was always willing to go the extra mile to ensure that the needs of the state administration were met and that the people of the state were well-served.

Once the list of state services officers was sent to him from the office of the Chief Minister and he was asked to issue the transfer order. In Tripura, this had become a practice The transfer of civil services officers was decided by the political party and then sent to the Chief Minister who would then get the order issued. Mr Damodaran was of the view that this was the prerogative of the bureaucracy as the civil servants should not be influenced by political ideologies. He did not issue the order received from the CM office for transfer. The CM did remind him on various occasions and asked him to issue the order. The delay in issuance of the order of the CM was not taken very positively by the political set up in the State. Once it became public that there had been a non compliance of the CM's order, he had to make a choice to continue as CS or convey the message of being just a rubber stamp of the political executive. He sacrificed his post of CS in view of this and similar other conflicts where he was trying to establish the neutrality of the state administration and insulate it from political interference.

Apt Handling of Stakeholders

Due to his cordial relation with other officials in the central government and his ability to convince, he could get approval for a large number of projects for the State. It was during his time that the state could get a large number of projects due to his ability to convince central Ministries. The Finance Commission team was so impressed by the presentation made by him that extra resources, the highest amongst the NE states, were received by Tripura ; this was only possible due to his efforts.

His ability to connect with people and his sharp acumen and vision soon caught the attention of the then Union Finance Minister. The Minister was so impressed with Mr Damodaran's abilities that he proactively recommended him for an important central posting. This was testament to Mr Damodaran's outstanding reputation and the high regard in which he was held by his peers.

His unwavering commitment and dedication to his job, despite the challenges and criticisms he faced, only served to reinforce his reputation as an exceptional civil servant. His tireless efforts and unwavering dedication to the people of the state are a true testament to his character and commitment to public service.

❑

Chapter 7

An Officer With A Unique Skill of Promoting People/ Entrepreneurs

– Dr Sabahat Azim

Ex-IAS Officer, founder of Glocal

M Damodaran, fondly called "D" by most who know him, is a living legend with diverse qualities of a great leader, motivator and team builder. For countless officers in the Indian Administrative Services, especially in the Manipur - Tripura cadre, he has been the inspiration and role model as an ideal Officer to emulate and imbibe the virtues of a Civil Servant. He embodies the qualities of an institution builder and a person of impeccable integrity. His life and the experiences one has while working with him cannot be described in a few pages. Some incidents are narrated herewith - not because of the content but because of my own limitations of writing skills. After the first 10 years of being in Government, I developed an aversion to writing. I guess I did enough note writing in my short career in the IAS to last a lifetime.

I joined the Tripura cadre and after a short stint in the field was posted as the secretary to the Chief Minister at a very young age. The post gave an opportunity to interact closely with the senior civil services officers in the State. Mr Damodaran's reputation as the Chief Secretary was generally remembered and everyone who has worked with him has great adulation and inspiration from his style of functioning.

A Management Guru Who Walks the Talk

D is not a person or an officer -he is a management book in himself. He is a guru who walks the talk. I think a better person than me can actually cull out a complete management treatise from his life as a civil servant. He is an example of not only how to build up or run an organisation but also how to do the right thing even while losing out on personal benefits. He has taught me how to build an organisation, how to pursue dreams and hold them dear even in adversity. After my father, who has taught me that life is beyond one's own personal needs, D has been the source of inspiration and support for me. To the little that I have achieved in my life, his sagacity and support have been like a rock(spiritual Guru) for me though the failures or mistakes have been my own.

In the year 2005, I was Secretary to the Chief Minister of Tripura, when Mr Damodaran was the Chairman of the Securities Exchange Board of India. He came to Agartala for the inauguration of the Branch of Stock Holding Corporation of India Ltd. The CM gave a speech which was finely nuanced between the political ideology of the ruling party (Communist Party of India - Marxist) and the imperatives of the country and the state, delineating the need for reforms and transparency so as to include every citizen in the emerging opportunities in the capital enterprise/market of the country. It was very well delivered and received. I was not present at the ceremony but I shortly received a call from Mr Damodaran from the Raj Bhawan, where he was staying, asking if I could be available for a cup of tea with him. I was a very junior officer and getting such an invitation itself was a shock, for he could have invited the Chief Secretary or other Secretaries who had worked with him. He knew that the speech prepared for the CM was the handiwork of a young officer and must have found out that it was drafted by me. More astonishing for him was that I was able to convince the CM (left ideology) to talk about promotion of capital markets in the State to empower citizens.

D was already a legend in the state, in the cadre to which he belonged where he had been the Chief Secretary years before and worked in many other positions/ departments. During his tenure at SEBI - for the first time SENSEX was doubling and quadrupling under his stewardship and by the time he left, it had grown 4X, the fastest growth of Sensex ever and a sign of the trust he had promised to investors about the Indian capital markets. Any junior in service would have given an arm and a leg to be invited to tea by him but he generally did not ask people to come and meet him. He said to me - a person 30 years his junior - almost fresh in service and with nothing yet to show in terms of accomplishments - "I was wondering that in your schedule, is it possible to get some time to have a cup of tea with you?" His grace and humility is simply unsurpassable and infectious - even though I have tried to learn from him but found it difficult to remove my rough edges during the last 18 years of my service in Government and outside (I resigned from IAS and became an entrepreneur) and aspire for "D"s level of competence/ capability.

An Inspiration for the Young

He builds up, promotes and encourages younger officers and gives them confidence to achieve their best. Surmising that I had some contribution to the speech, he told me - " The speech that the CM gave seemed like it could have been in the Wall Street Journal." While we cannot claim credit for the speeches of our leaders, it brings a glow to you when you hear the SEBI chief making such a comment. I am yet to see someone who can give you such a compliment with such finesse. No wonder he built up institutions. I once asked him if he could tell his story of turning around UTI and IDBI and building up SEBI – for capital market revival especially after the Harshad Mehta and Ketan Mehta scam. He said, "I don't do the work. The work is done by the team and my job is to enable them." I am not taking that at face value but the style of giving credit to his subordinates for everything, is also his hallmark. I have seen him personally and professionally, giving people the confidence that they can do things which are impossible and for those who have that faith and belief, it can do wonders. I have met many other people for whom his trust and faith gave them the fuel to fire their dreams. It is like the storyboard of Superman. He can fly because he is from another planet. The day reality comes close - like Kryptonite from his home planet - he loses his powers. It is the same for all of us. We are all ordinary mortals, when someone or something gives us faith and belief that this impossible thing can be done, we go about wholeheartedly doing it. It is the faith that we can do that makes us believe and that belief makes us do things that we otherwise would not have attempted. The parents who sent Superman to the Blue Planet were giving him the faith to fly while the naysayers like Lex Luthor were bringing Kryptonite to tell him he does not have any special powers. Young people wanting to change the world need faith givers like D to fly and that is his mojo and that is how he transformed organizations.

Supporting Spirit During Difficult Times

D consented to be the Chairman of my fledgling company just to enable an ambitious social project to bring services to the underserved. An Ex-SEBI chairman accepting to become the chairman of a startup with almost "nil" resources, except the technical expertise, was itself a great motivation for a young entrepreneur like me. He put in his own hard earned money only on the basis of trust and never asked where it was going or if there would be a return to him. It is hard to disrupt life's inequalities and when you face challenges, there are times when the going is so tough that you might be tempted to throw in the towel. It is in times like these that entrepreneurs may give up their dreams, but encouraging words spoken about your dream to a third person provide that much needed motivation to continue and grow.

In one such moment when I was faced with too many pending receivables and collections not happening, I was doubting the sustainability of the whole enterprise. I was thinking why I would have to take the responsibility of bringing affordable healthcare to people - I am not the Government and my life could be so much easier doing something already proven to be profitable or I could have remained in Government with security and comfort. That day someone called me and told me that he had met D at an airport and had asked him what India needed to develop and he had said that, "if we have 10 people like Sabahat, the country will change." Don't get me wrong - this isn't about me. It's about the good word. It's about building up young entrepreneurs, especially social entrepreneurs, who attempt to solve social problems. It's about talking about them and building them up. It is what leaders do in a good organization. It is what a nation's leaders do. If we fail to live up to the expectations then it's our fault but I was blessed by him and people like him who nourished my dreams and supported me through thick and thin. Today, he has played a big role in helping me build a sustainable social health care enterprise not only for India but for many other developing countries across the world.

Non Compromising on Compliance

While he was always generous with praise, he had a unique style of commenting about mistakes and his style was extremely effective. D has always been a stickler for propriety and doing the right thing. Sometimes he would insist on so many things that once another investor took me aside and said "you run the risk of being a company with 100% compliance and no business." He was frustrated with the time we took in Board meetings to review compliances and stuff. But D was right. In good times these things don't matter, but in bad times they really help you. His style of pointing out things is more effective. He will say "It might be a good idea to consider this..." rather than "you should do this." It prevents people from becoming defensive, but rather makes them amenable to see what can be done. It is a much better and effective management tool to help steer organisations on the correct path, rather than pointing out flaws and becoming an obstructionist in smooth functioning/ growth. Only people genuinely interested in good governance would try to enable, rather than force and it goes without saying that with him on the Board of a company, the company would always do the right thing -it may be a sign to blindly put in your money where D is on the Board of the company.

Always Support in Doing Right Things

As it happens in life, you would run into problems not of your own making but also sometimes get swindled or cheated by somebody more powerful and against whom you would not have the resources to fight back. In such a situation when you went to Mr Damodaran for advice, he would only say, 'do what is right, irrespective of the result'. This is rather frightening advice but I think it is the right advice - almost spiritual in essence - like the Geeta - "*karm karo, phal ki chinta mat karo*" - do your job without worrying about the results. However, I think in the larger play of the cosmos, it is probably right as we are all but actors in a play. Neither fear nor favour nor desire should prevent one from doing whatever is right and in that teachings of D may be 'right in his advice '. When you were a bit frightened of the consequences of standing up for what is right, and told him what had happened, he would smile and say - "this too shall pass." I asked him once when he wasn't given an extension of the tenure of SEBI stewardship despite the stellar role he had played and he had replied - "I have earned my right not to stand and wait for any Minister and that is a happy ending." So it is not that D is advising others to stick to something they believe is right without having done it himself. He has, I would say, earned the right to be a teacher – a practitioner before being a preacher; a very rare quality among civil servants.

A Great Motivator

His one-liners are a delight but that would require a complete book. I do think he might want to spend some time writing a book about management with each chapter beginning with one of his own one liners. It would be a great motivational book for entrepreneurs. When you are in difficulty – which happens in every one's life – his one-liners are a source of motivation and encouragement – they are something spiritual.

It is difficult to paraphrase his contribution to the country and I have focused only on the things I have learnt from him, but I would think that for many people in the public or private sphere he has been the coach, friend, philosopher and guide and if we probably calculate the sum total of jobs created, production done and value created by enterprises, departments, organisations mentored by him, his impact may be larger than anyone else. I hope he goes from strength to strength and keeps guiding entrepreneurs and leaders from all walks of life. It will be good for the country and for the people he coaches; for them the journey would be delightful. As for the companies where he continues to be director or advisor – one can trust those organizations to follow ethical practices and definitely be regulatory compliant.

❑

Chapter 8

My Association with Mr. Damodaran[1]

– G Sethu
Retd Professor & Dean, IIM, Tiruchirappalli

I have known Mr. Damodaran since the year 1982. I was allotted the Manipur Tripura cadre of IAS and while undergoing training at LBSNAA, Mussoorie, I had called on Mr Damodaran, who had also come to LBSNAA at the same time to attend another training program. If I remember correctly, at that time he was the Deputy Secretary to the Government of India and posted in New Delhi. Since he was from the same cadre, as per the practice and tradition (normally probationers would call on and meet officers of their cadre) I met him to get feedback about the cadre. This was my first meeting with him. He was very articulate and impressive and said very good things about the cadre, its work culture, ethics etc. After meeting him, I was very excited to join the Tripura cadre. He possesses excellent skills of motivating and exciting colleagues.

---

1 Sethu Gururajan, Retired Professor & Dean, Indian Institute of Management, Tiruchirappalli

Truly a Multi Tasker

The next time I met him, it was in Agartala. He was Secretary to many departments at the same time. As junior IAS officers from the sub-divisions and districts, we had the privilege of walking into the offices of senior IAS officers without any specific business to transact (Tripura culture). I used to go to his chamber to pay courtesy calls. I often found many officers sitting before him. He used to be busy clearing the files but at the same time would engage all the officers in conversation. He was able to listen to all of them and give guidance and instructions, never once taking his attention off the files. He was truly a multi-tasker! – unique skill amongst the civil servants.

I had left the IAS and moved into a teaching career. Later I went to Bombay to work with the UTI Institute of Capital Markets, established by the Unit Trust of India. I learned many things about UTI and about the securities markets. Mr. Damodaran was Joint Secretary in the Banking Division of the Finance Ministry. Whenever I visited New Delhi, I used to go to the Jeevan Deep Building in Connaught Place, where the Banking Division was housed, to meet Dinesh Tyagi (he was Director in the Banking Division) and Mr. Damodaran. One evening he asked me about US64. US64 was the short form of Unit Scheme 64, a very popular mutual fund scheme launched by UTI in 1964. Many individuals had invested in US64 as there were many attractive tax breaks/incentives. He said his father had made investments in US 64 and he asked me how the scheme was doing. I told him that the scheme was doing well and had given good returns to investors. The scheme was paying handsome dividends and had tax breaks. In a matter of three or four years, he was tasked with managing the great crisis on account of trouble in the US64. I observed his quick grasp of complexities of US64 within a very short period of a few weeks. The way he resolved the crisis in a short period is a great lesson in financial market crisis management.

Deep Understanding About Investor Behavior

Once in a meeting at SEBI, there was a discussion as to what kind of investment product is suitable for a small investor. I argued that small investors should invest in equity to some extent and the best way would be through systematic investment plan in an index fund. I pointed out the advantages of this suggestion. Mr. Damodaran, who was the SEBI Chairman, intervened and said that he agreed with me and that one of the main concerns was the transparency of performance of the investment. I hadn't thought about that! I realized how good his grasp of investor behavior was – an essential for designing and promoting a financial product.

Apt Handling of Parliamentary Committees

As UTI Chairman, he had to appear before the Parliamentary Committee many times. He was accompanied by a team of senior officers from UTI. These officers would carry the data and information pertinent to the committee hearings and help the Chairman, if needed.

A colleague of mine was a member of that team. He told me that Mr. Damodaran handled every question all by himself. The committee hearings would go on for hours. During one such situation, the Chairman of the committee had offered that if Mr. Damodaran desired, he could ask one of his colleagues to answer the questions as he might be tired. This is a rare privilege as people familiar with parliamentary committee proceedings would know. But Mr. Damodaran declined the offer. At that juncture, Mr. Mani Shankar Iyer, a member of the committee observed that senior IAS officers are trained at managing the parliamentary committees! His colleagues at UTI were in awe of Mr. Damodaran's grasp of the complex matter and the way he answered every question that was put to him by the committee.

Strong Supporter of Public Sector

Mr. Damodaran has great faith in the public sector. I will narrate a few examples. During the UTI crisis, he had prepared a plan of action. He asked me what the course of action should be. I told him that several people are suggesting that UTI should be sold to a private sector player. He looked at me and said, "I have not come here either to liquidate or to sell UTI to a private sector player." Later he had to convince many persons in the Government about his plan for UTI including the then Finance Minister Mr. Jaswant Singh. Mr. Damodaran had high regard for Mr. Jaswant Singh. He told me that Mr. Singh was a voracious reader and that he had a vast private library. He said that it is difficult to gift a book to Mr. Jaswant Singh as it is likely that he would have already read it! Mr. Singh was a quick decision-maker and would focus more on strategic issues leaving the details to the subordinates. Mr. Damodaran narrated to me what had happened during a presentation that he had made before the FM. He had presented a slide that showed the top ten mutual funds, showing the private sector in red colour and public sector in green colour. Only two mutual funds were in green, one was UTI and the other was SBI. Mr. Damodaran pointed out that if UTI was privatized, nine out of ten top mutual funds would be in the private sector! That settled the matter. The FM said "no" to privatizing the UTI! He has the unique ability to get approval for his approach and plan, of course when he is convinced that it is in the best interest of the institution and the country.

Once, during an interview, the reporter mentioned that the members of the cabin crew of private sector airlines were smart while members of the cabin crew of Indian Airlines were older and not so smart. Mr. Damodaran retorted saying that at 36,000 feet above ground, what we need are experienced and technically qualified crew members who can handle emergencies professionally! I think this respect for the public sector must have given him the drive and motivation to transform UTI and IDBI! I wish he was also given the opportunity to work for Indian Air lines – he would have really done something dramatic!

A Great Communicator

Everyone who knows Mr. Damodaran understands that he is a great communicator. I have learnt a great deal about good verbal and written communication. I was invited to make a presentation to the Board of Directors of UTI Asset Management Company regarding the incentive scheme for the portfolio managers. I made a technical presentation with graphs and equations. I left the board room after the presentation. During lunch, one of the directors told me that my presentation went over everybody's head. I felt foolish! The director said, "Your chairman explained in simple English that you were talking about a S shaped curve to decide the rewards. Immediately everyone understood and approved your suggestion." One had to learn from Mr Damodaran how complex issues can be explained in simple terms.

Very Witty

He has a great wit! I was in his office one evening and said "Sir, the files that come to you come without much scrutiny." He retorted, "Perhaps they are also going out without much scrutiny!"

When he was appointed as UTI Chairman, people in the Bombay financial markets did not know him. He was to arrive from New Delhi to Mumbai. The acting Chairman of UTI spoke to him over telephone and said that he would go to the airport to receive him but was wondering how to recognize him. He responded, "You may not have seen me before, but I see you on television everyday these days. I will locate you!"

Very Fast in Decision Making

When he came to SEBI as Chairman, he had spent less than four years in Mumbai's financial markets. However, he had figured out the intricacies of the market. He decided to strengthen the legal side of SEBI as the record of SEBI before the Securities Appellate Tribunal and courts was poor. The regulatory side of SEBI has improved to a considerable extent since then. His ability to declutter the matters resulted in speedy decision-making. In 2008, when his term at SEBI ended, a farewell function was organized. Late Ms. Usha Narayanan, then ED at SEBI mentioned that "under Mr. Damodaran's chairmanship it was regulation at the speed of SMS."

Respect for Juniors

Mr. Damodaran has the ability to build and maintain friendships. I think this is because of the genuine affection, respect and concern he shows for the people who work with him. When he was SEBI Chairman, he went to Washington D.C. to attend meetings of IOSCO in his capacity as the Chairman of the Emerging Markets Committee of IOSCO. He was scheduled to meet the SEC Senior official. One of my friends from Mumbai, who was working with USAID, was part of the team. Mr. Damodaran had invited him to go with him for the meeting with a SEC senior officer. When both of them reached the Office of SEC, the officer at the reception said that the appointment was only for Mr. Damodaran and, therefore, they could not permit entry to his companion. Mr. Damodaran told them that they would have to either admit both of them or he would not meet the SEC official. The officer at the reception had no alternative but to grant permission to the companion. My friend was greatly touched by this gesture! In contrast many senior officers in civil services do not take their immediate juniors to the meetings with senior officers or Ministers and ask them to wait in the ante room, even though there may not be explicit instructions to this effect.

I had an opportunity to interact with Late Justice Y.V. Chandrachud, former Chief Justice of India. He had made some investments in the UTI's US64. There was some problem relating to that. He once mentioned that to me. I conveyed it to Mr. Damodaran. Within a period of one or two days, Mr. Damodaran called me and asked me if I could arrange an appointment with Justice Chandrachud. He came to Justice Chandrachud's residence and very respectfully handed over some papers to him and told him that the matter had been resolved. When we were returning, I told him I could have done that duty and he need not have taken the trouble. He replied that it was not everyday that he got an opportunity to have tea with a former Chief Justice of India! That is the kind of respect he showed to high offices!

Often, he would tell me that institutions are bigger than individuals. Once there was a meeting at the SEBI conference room and I had the responsibility to oversee the logistics. I had arranged the meeting table and placed the nameplate of the Joint Secretary (Capital Markets) two seats away from the Chairman. Mr. Damodaran came to check things before the meeting. He noticed what I had done and asked me to arrange the seat of the JS next to the Chairman. I said that the other person whom I had placed next to the Chairman was much more senior than the JS. Mr. Damodaran told me that the JS represented the Government of India, and it did not matter if he was relatively junior!

Working With Him is Learning Every Day

I knew that Mr. Damodaran had worked with Dr.Y.V. Reddy either in the Banking Division or in the RBI. Once I asked him what the experience was like. He replied, "when you work with him, you learn something new every day." I can say the same thing about him. Late Dr. Pritam Singh interviewed me once for the book he was writing on leadership. He asked me to mention the animal that came to my mind when I thought of Mr. Damodaran. As a reflex action, I said "elephant." I must have intuitively referred to his grand personality, kindness and intelligence. Then Dr. Singh asked me to mention a bird that came to my mind. I thought for a long time, but I did not have an answer. After many years, it occurred to me that "Garuda", the celestial vahana of Lord Vishnu might have been appropriate!

He is a great teacher and a guide. He can motivate and get the best out of every one. It is a matter of great privilege for me and for all those who have had the opportunity to work with him or be associated with him.

❑

Chapter 9

An Untold Facet of His Towering Personality

– Dr A K Krishna Kumar
Ex Rubber Production Commissioner

There are few who cast a lasting impression: be it in one's personal or professional life. Mr. M. Damodaran is one of those rare individuals who not only influenced me, but also contributed immensely to my professional growth, in turn helping change the socio-economic landscape of one of the most backward and vulnerable regions of this country – Tripura in the North East.

Though I had heard about Mr Damodaran within the family circle much before any professional level interaction, I never had any opportunity to meet him. I was appointed as Deputy Director heading the north-eastern research complex of the Rubber Board (under Ministry of Commerce of Government of India) at Agartala (Tripura) in the year 1986. Though comfortably placed at the headquarters of the Rubber Board at Kottayam in Kerala, I still decided to accept the irresistible elevation and shift to Agartala with my wife and our 2 ½ year old twins. The move left many thinking that I had gone mad! Tripura was portrayed as a place rife with constant ethnic conflicts, insurgency and a volatile law and order situation that was further exacerbated by relatively less developed basic infrastructure with respect to health, schools, other civic amenities and so on. For anyone accepting a posting when offered alternatives, this would be definitely questionable.

Looking back, not only do I not regret the decision, but I consider it a blessing-challenges notwithstanding - as it turned out to be a training ground in conceptualising and implementing many initiatives without the stereotypical bureaucratic fetters, of course. One of the factors that bolstered my confidence, besides my own assessment based on a 40-day stint at Agartala on a temporary posting in the year 1982, was the reference of a couple of officers holding senior positions in the state and Mr Damodaran was one of them.

My first meeting with Damodaran was in June 1986 while he was the Revenue Commissioner. The meeting was regarding the implementation of one of the Rubber Board's flagship projects in the northeast, the Nucleus Rubber Estate and Training Centre (NRETC) for which about 1000 hectares of land was to be allotted by the State Government. Though a couple of sites were identified, the allotment ran into problems due to local resistance. Mr Damodaran took personal interest in the matter and though he left on deputation in 1987, he made sure to put in a word with some key officials that the needful has to be done. I was told by one of the senior officers in the forest department that Mr Damodaran had conveyed very categorically to all concerned that this shall be supported on priority as this was in the long term interest of the state and especially the Tribal people. My close association with him however started when he returned to the state in 1992 and was appointed the Chief Secretary there after. By that time, I had been appointed the Joint Rubber Production Commissioner - and was responsible for the development of the rubber plantation sector in Tripura.

The Rubber Board was in the process of implementing the "Rubber plantation development scheme" adopting strategies like those underway in Kerala. The socio, economic and cultural profile of potential rubber growers in Tripura being quite different, the plantations raised so far were far from successful, including the ones in the public sector. The worst performing plantations were the ones with tribal growers and for tribals raised by Government agencies. The very appropriateness of a technology-intensive crop like rubber - for tribals who formed about a third of the population and were most vulnerable - was being questioned. These views had already been expressed by the fact-finding missions of the World Bank Project team assessing the feasibility of supporting a large-scale rubber project in the country under which Tripura was also to be covered.

Looking at the adversities, the NRETC project was a non-starter, the scope of rubber plantation development for tribals being questioned and in spite of the fact that my key responsibility as Joint Rubber Production Commissioner (Jt RPC) was, the implementation of the NRETC, I had to justify the relevance of a Jt RPC rank official in Tripura!

In the meantime, a concept for economic resettlement of tribal shifting cultivators was conceptualised. This endeavour aimed at the convergence of funds from the State Government ear-marked for revitalisation of old tribal rehabilitation projects. The major objective of the project was to make good the lost opportunity of establishing an NRETC in Tripura, making use of the funds allocated for the same, demonstrating that rubber could be successfully grown, achieving near levels of productivity in the traditional growing region by tribals and proving that tribals can rise to the occasion if properly motivated, skilled and empowered.

Starting in just 4 tribal colonies in the year 1992, it later got extended to 54 colonies and further led to a massive adoption by small and marginal farmers in the state, especially tribal -shifting cultivators. In 1992 about 68% of the total area of 18250 hectares belonged to tribals and by the end of 2021, the total area under rubber cultivation in the state was close to 90,000 hectares with a production of about 94,000 tonnes annually (estimated value of raw rubber at current price is Rs. 1400 Crore), 80% of which is accounted for by tribals. This was possible with whole hearted support of Mr Damodaran who as a visionary appreciated the relevance of the extensive rubber plantation in Tripura especially for the upliftment of the Tribals. Earlier schemes of the State Government for tribal rehabilitation had very limited success and acceptance of Rubber plantation as an alternative (being a long gestation crop) was quite challenging

Support for A Unique InitiatIve for Tribal Rehabilitation

Nothing succeeds like success! The project later become one of the flagship schemes of the state which not only helped significant enhancement of income of small and marginal farmers and supported the state in moderating insurgency as endorsed by the former Chief Minister of the state in one of his interviews to a national newspaper (Recently, the Commerce Minister of the Government of India also wholeheartedly endorsed that Rubber plantation development helped curb insurgency in the region). Readers may wonder why I went into these seemingly unrelated details explaining a rubber project while sharing my experience of working with Mr Damodaran, who is known mostly for his stellar contributions in the financial sector of India. Though the Tripura stint is a small initiative, I thought it befitting to place on record his contributions in the right perspective. This is an initiative which had far-reaching ramifications and showed Mr Damodaran's unflinching support for a long term cause, which are not known to many.

I would also like to mention that the project had the patronage of several political leaders and officers whose involvement, right from its conception, contributed immensely to the success of this venture. However, there were crucial moments that needed the blessings of those holding the highest office and one cannot emphasise enough the fact that the project was launched while he was the Chief Secretary. They say 'well begun is half done'; to paraphrase a famous football reference, and that is what the 'hand of Damodaran Sir' did to this high-impact – unique project.

The project mentioned earlier was highly complex and given the many adverse conditions prevailing in the state, could not have had a smooth run. The fate of the project could have been entirely different; in which case, it could have been easily passed off as yet another tribal development project that failed due to factors beyond control. The project beneficiaries were rudimentary in terms of living, knowledge, education or means and were the least developed even among tribals, with temporary dwellings in remote, not easily accessible locations frequented by insurgents. To make matters even more challenging, these beneficiaries were being offered the choice of dealing with a perennial non-food crop with a gestation period of 7 years.

The project work commenced without any fanfare in the winter of 1991, followed by field-planting in the month of June 1992. Mr Damodaran, on his return from deputation, assumed the office of chief secretary in July 1992. I remember having met him to give an overview of the Board's activities, specifically the tribal development project. From thereon, the keen interest he took in this project shaped the performance of this project, which again, is not known to many. Although I had the unique opportunity to work closely with him, I was representing another organisation. Therefore, I would like to believe that my perception would not have suffered the 'bias' of a subordinate officer!

Simple, Clever and Humane Traits

I witnessed the professionalism, charisma, leadership qualities and above all, the humane traits of his style of functioning. He demonstrated a simple yet in many ways, a profound model of clever and courteous management when leading people. A project of this nature and scale would have been too small or insignificant for the Chief Secretary of a state but in all probability, he sensed the impact it would create. On a specific occasion, I remember he called me over the telephone and asked me to submit a proposal for 'energy plantations' in the tribal hamlets in which we were implementing the rubber project. Tribal families in all these colonies were fully dependent on firewood from forest – thus affecting the forest's natural vegetation. Rubber also would need firewood for smoking the sheets, albeit after 5 to 6 years; these proposed energy plantations would ease the pressure on forests for the energy needs of both the colonies and the rubber sheets in the future. Within a day, the proposal was submitted and approved and this initiative, an add-on if one can put it that way, turned out to be highly successful benefitting both the Tribals and the forest department. This is yet another incident that serves as a clear indication that Damodaran Sir was in the thick of things with respect to the developments within the project.

All these things might come across as business-as-usual for any development administrator. However, what stands out is the role played by Damodaran Sir in salvaging the project at a highly crucial juncture. Things were moving at quite a brisk pace and the extent of acceptance of the project among the local community, especially the tribals, was gaining strength by the day due to the implementation strategy that had laid a strong emphasis on "voice being heard'. Furthermore, the project also harnessed other initiatives like the provision of drinking water, link roads, health camps conducted by senior doctors (almost all of the beneficiaries noted that they were being examined by a senior doctor and a specialist for the very first time in their life and that too at their hamlet), creche for children, special nutrition, adult literacy, so on and so forth. Getting such convergence in the nick of time could not have been possible but for Mr Damodaran's direct and indirect support.

In all honesty, I liberally used my official as well as personal proximity to Damodaran Sir to get things done. It was then that disaster struck in the form of a brutal ambush on our project team by insurgents at Rajchandai, just one kilometre from Ramchandranagar Tripura State Rifles' camp and 13 kilometres from Agartala on the 25th of May 1993. It claimed 7 lives and seriously injured two officials. Though I was being reminded by my colleagues about the impending danger, I dismissed those on the premise that since the project is for the benefits of tribals none of the tribal insurgents would harm the project. Perhaps due to my inexperience, I overestimated and trusted the ideological proclamations of those insurgent outfits. This was a real dampener, to put it mildly. The whole scenario changed and project staff who were highly committed, sincere and passionate had their morale shattered. The Chairman of the Rubber Board had asked me to review the pros and cons of implementing the project; with a recently commenced World bank project for rubber development in the country focussing on tribals, the stakes were too high and a lot depended on the decisions about the way forward.

It was at this juncture that I had the opportunity to see Mr Damodaran at his subtle best and his leadership excellence that was truly beyond the realm of possibility, given the high-octane circumstances. I had to reach out to him not only in my official capacity but at a personal level too to tide over the crisis.The official sources from which one would expect help in such situations were rather lukewarm in their response and to a certain extent, they even trivialised the situation saying that these incidents are 'nothing out of the ordinary' in the region.

The pep talks by a senior political stalwart of the state to the project staff proved counterproductive and rather detrimental. This gentleman even went to the extent of stating that they too (politicians) had lost a significant number of members during their struggle to establish themselves in the state'!

Leading by Example and Aptly Resolving Complexity of Situations

In stark contrast, Mr Damodaran gave unflinching support and time to deal with this situation. What was heartening was that he led by example, taking the time to visit the project locations in remote areas and engaging in interactions with the staff and the beneficiaries, which turned out to be a morale booster. He took the initiative of speaking to the then chairman of the Rubber Board and assured all support on behalf of the State Government. His oratory skills and the dexterity with which he handles complex subjects are legendary and well known to all those who know him. A fair measure of this was evident in his handling of the World Bank missions. The Rubber Board was the main implementing agency of the World Bank assisted rubber project, and there was a component for the state government to implement. He took personal interest in hand-picking the best, high-performing officials for heading the state component and I can recall him discussing with me about the task and the job roles for on-boarding the right officer. It was these seemingly small steps which led to the success of the project. Nobody can deny the role played by him during his tenure as Chief Secretary in bringing about socioeconomic transformation of such magnitude in a state like Tripura. This may not catch one's attention when comparing his accomplishments during his post-Tripura days, be it at the UTI or at SEBI but my intention is to share my experience of working with him and highlighting his contribution to the readers about a totally different area which is in stark contrast to the fields which he is known to have excelled at.

I am in no way a competent authority to analyse the personality of Mr Damodaran. All I can say is that he has not been falsely modest or arrogantly boastful and that he has been amazingly successful! I am also not sure in which class of leaders he belongs to. My guess is a combination of Laissez faire and transformational!

A Voracious Reader

His accomplishments could be attributed, among many other factors, to luck or good fortune, which we refer to as *Bhagyam*. In Sanskrit and in other Indian vernaculars, *Bhagyam* means luck or good fortune given by *Bhagavan* (the Supreme Being), which all are not privileged to possess. Many years ago, a highly revered individual, a veritable sage (who never met Mr Damodaran) chanced upon his horoscope by a strange turn of events, and confided in me that this horoscope was that of an *Utthampurushan* (the perfect man). I needed no further explanation on why he is so. What comes to me is the Shakespearean quote “Some Are Born Great; Some Achieve Greatness; Some have Greatness Thrust Upon Them”. All the three are applicable in Mr Damodaran’s case. Born to an illustrious judge with an aristocratic lineage, coupled with his amazing skills of switching roles with ease- bureaucrat to corporate honcho to thorough professional -one cannot expect the ordinary from him. I hasten to add that there has been a lot of effort put in by him in gaining a deeper understanding of subjects he has been dealing with and that helped him command respect. Besides being a voracious reader, he kept abreast of developments across the globe and took care to see that he achieved mastery in the field he has been working in. These are the qualities you rarely see particularly among bureaucrats. In fact, apart from other qualities mentioned earlier it is this quality which puts him head and shoulders above many belonging to his parent service.

I must also mention that his success must be attributed to the 'woman behind the man.' Also hailing from a family of diplomats, Mrs Damodaran, who also happens to be closely known to us, has contributed immensely to his long list of accomplishments. It is said that *Saraswati*, the Goddess of wisdom (and eloquence) and Lakshmi, the Goddess of wealth do not dwell together at the same place; but it seems that they have made an exception in the case of Damodaran Sir. By all counts, he is a towering personality. I stand witness to many of his colleagues, especially junior officers and those fresh out of the Academy (LBSNAA), attempting an adoption of his style with most of them ending up as poor imitators! I must admit, I too have tried to adopt some of his style, but with little success. In this day and age, he is one of a rare breed of professionals who are few and far between. We need him to play another long innings. With all humility and prayers, I wish him a long, happy and healthy professional life.

❑

Chapter 10

As a Chairman of a Company and Financial Professional

– Anil Parasher

It was at a Big-4 Governance seminar, post the fireside chat between Mr Damodaran and a senior international partner, that a young lady while asking a question mentioned that till then she had read about Mr Damodaran in general knowledge books. This pretty much sums up the aura and respect Mr Damodaran commands in the industry across all corporate professionals and all age groups! People throng to hang on to every word uttered by him. Mr Damodaran truly follows the adage 'Knowledge is of no value unless you put it into practice.'

I had been a member of Mr Damodaran's fan club for many decades before I met him in person. As a finance professional, I followed Mr Damodaran at various forums, savouring the vast expanse of knowledge, laced with anecdotes and his trademark wit! He stands at the very top where public speaking is concerned with a rare ability to articulate complex issues in his inimitable style! Where Mr Damodaran is concerned it's always '*Yeh Dil Maange More*'.

Professionalism Unparalleled and Exemplary

In early 2019, to my delight, Mr Damodaran was appointed as the Chairman of the Board of a company where I was a member. It was here that I came to know him personally! For me this was indeed a great blessing, as one rarely gets a chance to work closely with people whom one admires or who are their role model. I always looked up to him as someone from whom one can always learn about every aspect of life - both professional and personal. Board meetings were quite an experience, a combination of great discussions with a fair sprinkling of pressures and frustrations! Mr Damodaran navigated the meetings effortlessly, raising the bar time and again! He expected fellow directors and management to have read all the relevant documents and active participation was the rule. The company secretary carried the voluminous Companies Act to cope with Mr Damodaran's searching questions. 'Cometh the hour, cometh the man' could not be more true. There were occasions where the situation in the Board meeting due to conflicting interest and diverse opinions looked difficult to resolve but for the clarity, persuasive skills and witty skills of the chairman who handled them without hurting anyone - following the mantra of what was in the best interest of the organisation. His professionalism was unparalleled and exemplary.

His remarks on Quarterly monitoring and reporting about the financials of the company - "*Quayamat se Quayamat Tak*" is often quoted in regulatory bodies and industry circles looking for forbearance from these regimes.

Encourages Inclusiveness

Mr Damodaran, despite his calm demeanour, is always in command of the situation. To my mind, this stems from a complete understanding of the regulatory framework and great technical strength. Mr Damodaran encourages 'inclusiveness' by giving opportunities to every member to express their views freely. Additionally, in a single conversation, he can quote Keats, Longfellow, the Upanishads, cartoon publications, sports and music with aplomb. Despite the visible aura, Mr Damodaran remains a simple man, carrying his own chamomile tea bags.

During 2019 a 'Governance & Regulatory Conclave' was organised by Mr Damodaran's Excellence Enablers. Mr Kumaramanglam Birla reminded the audience that Mr Damodaran cited '*Mere Angne Mein Tumhara Kya Kaam Hai*' when the erstwhile Government wanted to meddle with SEBI during his tenure as the Chairman. On another occasion, when a couple of members made up, Mr Damodaran instantly came up with 'Ch*orho Kal ki Baaten, Kal ki Baat Purani*.' He always seems to have an apt response for every occasion. Getting the best out of the system without compromising on the basic ethics and governance principles is a unique quality of Mr Damodaran.

Mr Damodaran's interest in sports is epic, especially football and cricket! Despite a packed schedule, he carves out time to watch an IPL match in the evening followed by a Manchester United contest in the middle of the night!

Mr Damodaran's intellectual capabilities can be gauged from the fact that he proudly recalls that he is an accidental IAS (and went on to reach the highest positions in the Government) after initially joining IIT for Engineering and dropping out after a year.

Mr and Mrs Damodaran are gracious hosts. Over the last 4 years, I have had the honour to visit their home and enjoy the freshly made sandwiches and vadas, always accompanied by a big box of an amazing collection of teas. I am blessed to have always got time from Mr Damodaran, even on the weekends.

Multi Tasking Skills

I have observed that even Sundays are packed days for him. I always wonder how he manages hectic travelling schedules, while finding time to spread knowledge through various talks, seminars and writings which have impacts on corporate and professional India. He possesses the rare acumen of efficiently managing and multi-tasking activities without an iota of tension or disturbance.

In many ways, Mr Damodaran remains an enigma...an extremely sophisticated man with a simple lifestyle!

Abraham Lincoln said 'In the end, it's not the years in your life that count. It's the life in your years,' and Mr Damodaran packs quite a punch!

Wishing Mr and Mrs Damodaran a happy and blessed life.

❑

Chapter 11

A Reformer of the Financial Sector

– MBN Rao
Ex CMD Indian Bank

Damodaran is a born leader and bound to achieve greater heights of excellence in whichever areas he chooses. I am not saying this today, after watching his achievements in life. My association with him started in April 1970, when I started my career as a banker. We belonged to the first batch of Probationary Officers of Indian Bank, post nationalization, and even during our induction training, all of us realized that such a brilliant person like Damodaran would go places and it was just a matter of time before he would take up more challenging and fulfilling assignments. He is brilliant in more ways than one. We all admired his exceptional clarity, logic, creativity and articulation skills on diverse subjects. At the same time, he was very polite, soft spoken and friendly with his endearing smile. These are qualities that he has retained and continues to nurture irrespective of the top levels he has reached in many fields.

During training, all of us were required to speak on a chosen topic, and another Probationary Officer (PO) was required to introduce the subject and the speaker. Most of the POs had chosen simple topics in Banking or Economy. I was fortunate that I was selected to introduce Damodaran and give a brief of the topic chosen by him. While I knew something about Damodaran, I didn't know a bit about the topic chosen by him. I humbly requested him to explain the topic, and he was very kind and patient in explaining what it was and the nuances of the same. It was something like .... "The relevance of Realism in Indian Movies". Most of my fellow POs were wonderstruck with his articulation, language and analysis. No other topic selected by others came anywhere near Damodaran's talk. We all looked up to him with admiration. We all moved to our next postings, and a short while later, we came to know that Damodaran had moved to SBI and sometime later he became an IAS officer. While all of us felt very happy about his achievement, we had a tinge of sadness that we had to miss him and his brilliance. But destiny has different plans, we know only as it unfolds.

Several years later, we came to know that Damodaran had moved to the position of Joint Secretary, Banking Division, Ministry of Finance, GOI. As JS, Banking Division, Damodaran was 'incharge" of Banking Operations (Supervision), laying policies for Banks and Financial institutions, and representing GOI, as owners of Banks. He had close interaction with Banks and introduced a lot of measures to improve the efficiency of the Banks. At that time all PSBs were 100% owned by GOI. Only Banks' CMDs and EDs had direct access to him.

A Practical Administrator and A Thinker

Damodaran has been a hands-on practical Administrator. He knew that NPAs problem had been part of banking activities and it needed some structural interventions. He strengthened the recovery mechanism by taking various effective measures. NPAs were a charge on the profitability of banks warranting increasing capitalization in banks and he thought of additional institutional measures, and observed steps taken by other counties for addressing the NPAs. Introduction of Asset Reconstruction Companies (ARCs) in India, to tackle the problem of NPAs was his brainchild. Now ARCs are part of our financial system, which shows his foresight. He enabled the setting up of a committee to study the system of ARCs and come up with recommendations for setting up ARCs. Indian Bank was one of the Banks grappling with the problems of NPAs, provisioning and the need for additional capital. Damodaran included the names of Srivastava IAS, GOI nominee on the board of Indian Bank and myself along with executives from other institutions, in the Committee constituted to study ARCs. Damodaran has deep understanding and insight into the working of financial systems in various developed and developing countries, which has been his great asset while handling various responsibilities in the Financial Sector. During the working of the Committee, Damodaran used to provide abundant guidance and insight, despite his busy schedule. While he had initiated the process of introduction of ARCs in India, he used to repeatedly convey his vision that ARCs sponsored by banks should not be self-perpetuating institutions and they should have an expiry label so that banks become more efficient in Risk Management, Credit Management, Monitoring, and Recovery. This philosophy is very clear, crucial and important for effective ARC structure. Successive individuals heading the Regulatory Organizations are echoing the views of Damodaran, that Banks need to be self-reliant in Risk Management. Bankers should remember that it was Damodaran who had initiated the process of introduction of ARCs in India to help the banks, with a vision that banks should improve Risk Management processes and practices.

Staunch Supporter of Social Banking

Damodaran appreciated the contribution made to social banking by PSBs. He has been a staunch supporter of social banking and financing to the downtrodden to promote social justice. It is not out of any isms, but out of the belief that when the less privileged sections of the community are taken care of there will be all round prosperity, social harmony and stability. When he was JS, Banking, he had come across reports by various committees sponsored by private entities, recommending closure and winding up of 'weaker PSBs'. Taking them as the basis, some officials of International Institutions used to call on him to get endorsement of such action. Mr Damodaran always maintained that those banks had been instruments of social change and had done well in the past and any aberrations should not be attributed to the entire institutional framework of PSB in India. He was instrumental in developing that clarity in saving long established institutions and protecting the interests of unconnected employees.

A Visionary Par Excellence

It is not out of place to mention that some of those 'weaker banks' are among the strongest banks now. For example, the revival/performance strategy of Indian Bank was largely based on the thinking and approach enunciated by Damodaran and has been followed the world over during the financial crisis of 2008 as well as in the ALM mismatch crisis in 2023. Damodaran has been a visionary, par excellence; time has only proved and reiterated that what he believed in and followed has been the right/ appropriate path in the Indian context.

Damodaran has been a great motivating and supportive leader. We, in Indian Bank, had felt in 1970, when he moved to take up more challenging roles, that we were deprived of the brilliant leadership of Shri Damodaran. But God had other plans. Indian Bank faced a peculiar situation in the year 2000, after the retirement of then CMD, and ED moved out on promotion, and with the completion of the term of majority of non-executive directors, the Board did not have quorum to meet, and take business decisions. That left the Bank topless. Ministry of Finance, GOI had appointed Shri Damodaran as OSD of Indian Bank, to oversee the working of Indian Bank, in addition to his existing responsibility of JS, Banking, MOF. Indian Bank employees, who had been facing very hard times, were overjoyed that such a senior functionary from MOF, who had earlier worked in Indian Bank, would head the Bank in a leadership role.

Employees of the Bank, most of whom believed in the supernatural power of the Almighty, felt that it was more than a coincidence and it was divine intervention. When Damodaran visited the Bank, there was a festive atmosphere, with employees thronging to see Damodaran. Damodaran met senior executives and conducted a meeting of the executives, listed out the plan of action and motivated them into taking decisions /action. All Indian Bank employees should be forever grateful to Shri Damodaran and Shri Dinesh Tyagi, IAS, GOI nominee on the Board of the Bank for the trust they reposed in the officers and employees of the Bank.

Shri Damodaran and Shri Dinesh Tyagi discussed, decided and appointed the 'Committee of GMs' to take care of the day-to-day operations of the Bank. They also motivated the members of the committee of GMs to ensure smooth operations of the Bank including decision making and assured their full support. Perhaps it would have been the only instance in the history of PSBs where the Banking Division, under the leadership of Shri Damodaran had taken such a step to ensure that the wheels of the Bank would keep moving. But for the bold step taken by them, the Bank would have collapsed, not because of the burden of NPAs, but because of the loss of public confidence, if decision making came to a grinding halt. I was directed to be the Member convenor of the Committee of GMs. It is with deep gratitude, on behalf of all the employees of the Bank, that I acknowledge that such initiative and support from both Shri Damodaran and Shri Dinesh Tyagi were unprecedented and unparalleled. In the very first meeting of the Board, when it was reconstituted by GOI, all the decisions taken by the committee of GMs were ratified by the full Board. It had given a tremendous boost to the confidence and morale of the organization.

Distress / Difficult Institution Turnaround Man

Shri Damodaran has been a great expert in organizational turnaround and possesses major ingredients/tools of turnaround. He maintains that Corporate Governance and Leadership are important factors. He practises what he believes in, while helping the turnaround of weaker Banks during very crucial periods. Damodaran ensured that very good professionals with proven track records were selected for Board positions. There were experts in credit risk like former MD of SBI and Former CEO of ICICI Bank, Experts in Technology and Management like serving and former Directors of IITs and CAs with impeccable reputation. There were a number of CBI cases against serving executives, which impacted decision making in Indian Bank. Damodaran was so very thoughtful that he managed to get a former Joint Director of CBI on the Board of the bank.

Then came the important issue of choosing competent and suitable persons to the CMDs role. A Search Committee was constituted and Damodaran ensured that very competent, energetic and dynamic leaders were chosen to head the weak banks to carry forward the restructuring and Turnaround of weaker PSBs. The specially chosen persons to take up the role of CMDs in weak PSBs have made exceptional contributions to the turnaround of the weak banks. In the case of Indian Bank, the search committee had to walk the extra mile to find the suitable man, and as famously quoted by Shri Damodaran, they identified a suitable person, and requested Mrs. Ranjana Kumar to lead the Bank. She made extraordinary contributions to the turnaround of the Bank. I was initially to be posted to Union Bank of India as ED, and after further discussion, I was posted to Indian Bank as ED. After Mrs. Ranjana Kumar moved to NABAARD as Chairperson, I was posted as CMD of Indian

Bank. Shri Damodaran has played a very prominent role in the remarkable turnaround of weak banks.

A Great Supporter for Integrity

Shi Damodaran, known for his uprightness, has stood by many honest officers of banks and was always ready to help them. He handled many sensitive legal matters at the highest level in the Supreme Court. He has also protected many executives of banks from undue pressures in decision making. Damodaran's association with the Banks and Financial Services Industry continued to the best advantage of the Financial Services sector/ industry.

In 2001, Damodaran was appointed the Chairman of UTI to rescue India's largest and oldest investment institution, which had collapsed. He restored UTI to health in arguably the most successful turnaround story in Indian financial sector history. Damodaran was simultaneously given charge of IDBI, another of India's major financial institutions. There, he created the Stressed Assets Stabilisation Fund, which helped clean IDBI's books, facilitating its conversion to a commercial bank and its merger with another bank.

Passionate about Improving Customer Service

Damodaran's passion for customer service is well known. He was also the Chairman of Reserve Bank of India's Committee on Customer Service in Banks. He has recommended active involvement of the boards of banks to guarantee customer satisfaction. "Commitment to hassle-free service for customers under the oversight of the bank's board is necessary to ensure maximum customer satisfaction. Customer centricity should be the purpose of the existence of the bank." The committee has said that customer service and grievance redressal should be included as a mandatory parameter in the performance appraisal report of all employees and it was introduced in all banks for the first time.

Damodaran's committee said, "The root cause analysis of the top five types of complaints in a quarter should be placed before the Customer Service Committee of the Board". The committee said that every Bank Board should ensure that they have comprehensive policies for customer acceptance, care and severance. The bank policies should clearly lay out its approach to customer care, taking into account the geographic spread of its branches, segments of customers, needs of special sections like senior citizens, widows, physically challenged persons, etc. The policy must also clearly define and distinguish the features for different products and services and must indicate the target customer group. It should show sensitivity for small customers by ensuring that the pricing (bank charges) does not act as a deterrent for the small person to do banking transactions.

Emphasising on 'customer centricity', the committee recommended that bank boards should evolve human resources policies which will "recruit for attitude and train for skills."

It pointed out that a policy should be framed to ensure that the prescribed response time for every type of grievance should be approved by an official not below the rank of the top management of the bank. Branch Level Customer Committee meetings may be replaced with a meeting of customers of all banks of that area (say district-wise, block-wise) and be held in the presence of representatives of banks at periodic intervals (monthly/quarterly). The responsibility of organising such meetings may be entrusted to eminent consumer organisations in the region and expenses of such meetings can be shared by the bankers of that jurisdiction. The proceedings of the meetings should be recorded (CCTV) for the purpose of review of the same in higher fora.

Damodaran was also Non-Executive Chairman of ING Vysya Bank, which was later merged with Kotak Mahindra Bank. Shri

Damodaran was also associated with Dutch financial services giant ING as its chief representative and advisor in India and played a significant role in growth of these institutions besides imbibing the values and ethos of Indian culture in their working.

Damodaran gives importance to good governance and has expressed on various fora that the Indian banking system laid with governance lapses needs a complete overhaul. Even now, he guides Bank Managements on Governance matters. Damodaran is very fond of his banker friends and gives his unbiased views with clarity.

❑

Chapter 12

Damodaran – A Memorable Innings at IDBI

– Jitender Balakrishnan

Around September 2003, there were rumours of a new CMD taking over the reins of IDBI. The name of Mr. M. Damodaran was being widely heard as to be given dual charge of IDBI and UTI, where he was already Chairman.

IDBI, the venerable old Institution was once the foremost Financial Institution (FI) in the Country, the Lender of the Last Resort, the Lead Institution of the Consortium of IDBI, ICICI, IFCI, UTI, LIC, and GIC. The Institution was responsible for laying the foundation of SEBI, and later had been given the task of setting up an Electronic Exchange and as part of that mandate had promoted the National Stock Exchange (NSE). It was responsible for promoting the National Securities Depository Ltd (NSDL), Stock Holding Corporation of India Ltd (SHCIL) and also a Rating Agency- CARE. It had earlier in the 80s carved out its Export- Import Division into the EXIM Bank (India) Ltd and thereafter in 1988 set up the Small Industries Development Bank of India Ltd (SIDBI) and in 1995 its own commercial Bank, IDBI Bank Ltd. The World scenario especially in the context of business operations was undergoing radical changes in the nineties and by the turn of the century, IDBI, as the unique infrastructure financing institution, had seen its influence waning.

I was Executive Assistant to Mr. SS Nadkarni, former chairman ICICI and later IDBI. In late 1993 as he prepared to take over as Chairman of SEBI, I remember him telling me,"I worry about IDBI, the world is changing, the way we do business is changing, internally the staff of IDBI has opposed many of the changes initiated. The leadership and staff. refuse to take blinkers off their eyes. Believe me, by the turn of the century, IDBI will have ceased to be relevant."

It was true that the staff had in 1993 gone on strike opposing structural changes in IDBI. In 1999 when the SH Khan Report was discussed, IDBI leadership with its remuneration linkages to RBI, had opposed IDBI's conversion into a Commercial Bank, while ICICI decided to convert itself into a Commercial Bank and finally merge with ICICI Bank in 2001. The decision of IDBI at the time to continue as a Financial Institution was disastrous. In 1997 IDFC had been set up to fund Infrastructure Projects, a forte of IDBI. Commercial Banks had been allowed into Term Lending like IDBI. To have a level playing field with Commercial Banks, Tax Concessions enjoyed by IDBI were withdrawn.

Borrowings by IDBI from Banks were no longer considered as priority sector lending. IDBI had to resort to Market Borrowings and without the benefits of CASA as available to Banks, cost of funds for lending became very competitive.

IDBI also had to follow Prudential Norms as applicable to Commercial Banks. Earlier the Financial Institutions, because of the high-risk developmental nature of their lendings, were allowed to convert 10% of their loans into equity of the concerned corporates at par over the currency of the loan. This boon available to FIs was withdrawn in mid 90s to be in line with SEBI Guidelines. This withdrawal was a major hit to IDBI's lending model, as for all practical purposes, IDBI was akin to a large venture capitalist.

By 2003, IDBI was at the cusp of a transitional stage in its history. Morale of employees was at a low. The FI had lost most of its renowned clients and loan assets to competition. To add to the pain, the CMD at the time had, while holding on to interest rates, declared to the Board that henceforth IDBI would assist only "A" and above rated clients. The joke in the market was that IDBI had stopped lending. This background is necessary to explain the context in which IDBI was at the time when Mr Damodaran took over. Many Pundits had already written its obituary and the morale of the employees was abysmal.

A strong hand was required to steer the Institution. Some of us in IDBI really hoped that the rumor of M.Damodaran taking over the reins of IDBI would come true. He had, as Chairman of UTI, restored that ailing Institution to health - a case study of a remarkable turnaround. He had the reputation of an able and efficient administrator with sharp acumen.

It was in this situation that Melevettil Damodaran took additional charge as CMD, IDBI from October 2003. He walked in bold, confident and a person with a no-nonsense approach. He was a man with a vision to fulfil. Seeing him, I remembered having met him once when he was Joint Secretary in the Ministry of Finance (MOF) to discuss issues relating to the Steel industry in India. He had gone into depth to understand nuances of various steel making processes, types of raw materials like ores, coal, coke, and their cost implications. He was not only a keen listener, but his ability to absorb and analyze vast amounts of data was phenomenal. I had come out of that meeting, amazed at his ability to incisively ask the right questions.

Instead of wasting time on niceties, his first action was to call a meeting of the senior leadership of IDBI. He was very focused. What were the issues IDBI was facing, what were the possible solutions in the short term and in the long term. We told him that IDBI had lost market share, it was also facing stress in some of its loan assets. Its high lending rates were not in conformity with the market combined with a Policy of selective and restrictive lending- only to A and above rated clients had impacted the business and growth.

Earlier CMD had made us lose many of our esteemed clients. Of the ten largest clients in our Portfolio, we had lost almost eight. Our loan assets had shrunk. We were also facing issues of stressed assets. In a courageous move which most Chiefs would not have taken in the first month of heading an organization, Mr Damodaran went to the Board and reduced Interest rates, if I recall, by 300 basis points. This was unprecedented. At the Board lunch, as I passed by him, he turned to me and said: -"it is the turn of you chaps now to deliver."

Always Looked at the Big Picture

I went to every high rated Corporate I knew, pleading that they come back to IDBI. I was told that our rates, though reduced, were still not competitive. I reminded them of their past relationship with IDBI, the support the Institution had extended to them and that everything should not be reduced to commercial terms. I said I understood that we may not be able to meet market rates but sincerely requested, that they allow us a rate 0.5% above the Market. HDFC Ltd was the quickest to oblige and I took a loan proposal from HDFC Ltd to the Board. CMD Damodaran and the Board were apprehensive of the interest rate we had proposed. I explained to the Board that this was HDFC, a Triple A rated Company. It was necessary from the point of view of Rating Agencies to have such companies in our Portfolio. Our Asset base would improve. The Board was not convinced but left it to CMD Damodaran to decide. IDBI had a function that evening and I recall Mr. Deepak Parikh, Chairman HDFC, who was at the function, asked me if the IDBI Board was happy with HDFC's quick response. At a loss for words, I told him there were some loose ends to be tied up and I would get back to HDFC the next day. He gave me a quizzical look but didn't say anything.

The next morning, we heard from the CMD's office that the proposal was unlikely to find favor unless the proposed interest rate was raised. I said it would not be possible as HDFC was a Triple A rated company and the interest rate proposed was already above market. I called my team to discuss the issue and we decided to put up a note justifying the proposal, the benefits that would accrue, and strongly recommending it. Quite apprehensive, I was pleasantly surprised when the note was returned that evening duly approved.

My respect for CMD Damodaran went up a couple of notches. Here was a true leader who saw the big picture, was not only willing to listen to his subordinates, but was ready to support them. It was precisely at that moment that I knew that Mr. Damodaran would make a huge difference to IDBI. In no time high rated corporate groups like the Tata Group, Reliance, Aditya Birla, Gujrat Ambuja and other MNCs responded to our request and were back in our portfolio.

Choosing the Right Man

Mr Damodaran took another step, to address the issue of NPAs. While we had all heard of the Good Bank- Bad Bank concept, one had not tried it out in India. Mr Damodaran was willing to take a calculated risk. He was instrumental in creating the Stressed Assets Stabilization Fund (SASF), a special purpose vehicle to clean up the Balance Sheet of IDBI. It was a masterstroke on the part of Mr. Damodaran, and he was able to convince the Government, RBI, and other Regulators to transfer Stressed Assets of Rs 9000cr from IDBI to SASF with strategic support from the Government. This cleaned up the Balance sheet of IDBI, paving the way for better ratings and cheaper borrowings. Mr. Damodaran also had the unique ability to choose the right man for the job. He chose Mr. Siby Antony, CGM who was virtually on his way to resign from IDBI. A dedicated team under Siby focused on arriving at a resolution of stressed assets in SASF and by 2008 the response was so good, that there were even discussions to close the fund.

Mr. Damodaran turned his attention next to the large, stressed assets in IDBI's Books, like Essar Oil Ltd (EOL) and Dabhol Power Plant (Dabhol). He called me one evening and asked me if EOL was in my Portfolio and whether I knew anything about it. He said ICICI was considering restructuring the asset and lending further money to fund cost overrun and complete the Project. I said that it was not a part of my portfolio, but I believed EOL had good potential and needed to be revived. He surprised me by requesting me to meet Mr. KV Kamath, Chairman ICICI and handle the project henceforth. Essar Oil was implemented and went on to become a crown jewel in the Essar stable.

Full of Throwing Surprises – Unpredictability as an Essence

It was always difficult to assess what Mr. Damodaran would do next. On one occasion after a Board meeting, he rang me up and asked if I was free and would join him for dinner at The President Hotel. I was thrilled. It was not every day that the CMD of IDBI invites a lowly CGM for dinner. I rang up the CMD's office but they didn't seem to be aware of any dinner. I went to the Hotel at 7pm but did not find Mr. Damodaran. I waited in the lobby for some time wondering if I had heard Mr. Damodaran correctly. Soon I saw Kalpana Morparia, Exec Director, ICICI and a team from ICICI walking in. We exchanged pleasantries. They said that they were having a meeting on Dabhol with Mr.

Damodaran. More Bankers came in including the IDBI's Dabhol Team led by IDBI Exec Director AK Doda. By now I was thoroughly confused about the dinner with Mr. Damodaran. He walked in then and seeing me, asked me to join the meeting. I told him that I was not involved with Dabhol and I was there as he had called me for dinner. He said that was fine, but requested me to join the meeting. I found a place in one corner of the room. Mr. Damodaran started the meeting and pointing at me he said, "I suppose you all know JB. He will handle Dabhol henceforth, reporting directly to me."

That was Mr Damodaran. He was full of surprises, but every action conveyed a message, left unsaid. As a prominent Industrialist once said "Mr Damodaran believes in the Policy of "shock and awe. "

The initiatives taken in IDBI by Mr. Damodaran during 2003 and 2004 would pave the way for revival of stressed assets and help to take advantage of the economic boom that was to follow.

On May 31, 2004, Mr. Damodaran was reappointed CMD, IDBI to hold office till May 31, 2007. In June 2004 he sent for me. He asked why I was not reporting to him. I replied that I had been reporting to the concerned Executive Director (ED). He asked me whether I had been called for an interview. I said that in the last two years, interviews called for the post of ED had been postponed for extraneous reasons. Within a few weeks, some of my colleagues and I were called to face an interview board. After a rather tough and gruelling session with the Interview board, I found myself promoted to the position of Executive Director and given charge of the most important portfolio of Corporate Finance. I went to meet Mr. Damodaran and thank him for the faith he had reposed in me. I told him that I didn't know what I had done to deserve the heavy Corporate Portfolio that he had put me in charge of. He said something which has remained etched in my memory.

He said "You have been given IDBI's very demanding and important corporate portfolio not for your past performance but for the potential you have, to revive and grow the portfolio". I was as always, awed by Mr. Damodaran's deep strategic thinking and his firm resolve to go ahead with what he believed in. I was reminded of another CMD who would rather procrastinate than take a firm decision.

Very Firm and Decisive

Mr. Damodaran's firmness in his beliefs came to play on another occasion. The IDBI Board had approved a restructuring proposal, but a majority of the Board members felt that the Chairman of the Company should be asked to step down and an independent professional be given the reins. Mr. Damodaran strongly felt that considering the complexity of issues involved, it would be in the stakeholders' interest to have the promoter Chairman with his considerable business acumen and experience to oversee the restructuring and completion of the project, rather than a professional with no stake in the project. He was able to convince the Board and later events were to prove Mr. Damodaran right.

Always Set High Expectation / Targets

Mr. Damodaran had by now a grip on IDBI operations and was fully focused on reviving it. He had a Vision for IDBI, and he was relentlessly implementing it. I recall when a reporter once asked him if he was trying to catch up with ICICI which was then the 3rd largest bank in terms of assets, and his answer was that he only benchmarked with SBI, the No 1 Bank in the country.

He started laying the foundation for the eventual merger of IDBI and its subsidiary IDBI Bank. There were Regulatory issues like meeting Regulatory norms as prevailing in a Commercial bank where IDBI may be required to seek dispensation. Considering the various issues involved and IDBI's Constitution, it was felt that initially one may need to set up a Holding company under Company Law. The erstwhile Industrial Development Bank of India was incorporated as a Government Company under the Companies Act 1956 on 27 September 2004. Thereafter the undertaking was transferred to and vested in IDBI Ltd with effect from 01 October 2004. The Entity would have 2 SBUs one for Commercial Banking with IDBI Bank (into which IDBI Home Finance would be merged) while the 2nd SBU would continue to focus on Project financing and Development banking. Mr. Damodaran with his understanding of the Government and knowledge of RBI, SEBI and the Financial System was indeed a boon for IDBI during these difficult times. (Any other person would have found it difficult to convince the various stakeholders)

No Nonsense Approach

Mr. Damodaran led IDBI from the front. At UTI he had orchestrated a remarkable turnaround. With him at the helm, IDBI was able to clean its books with the setting up of the SASF. He facilitated IDBI's conversion into a commercial bank and merger with another bank. His no nonsense approach to resolving issues brought him support from the Staff who saw in him the ability to bring back IDBI to its former glory. During his tenure in IDBI he introduced a Voluntary Retirement Scheme and strategically used it to move out deadwood and those that did not have a commitment to the Institution. His ability to communicate was tremendous. When he spoke, his clarity of thought was such that it conveyed to each what was required to be done without any ambiguity. He was firm but fair in his dealings.

Great Oratory Skills

His oratory skills were spellbinding. I recall some time after he had retired as Chairman, SEBI, I was sitting next to him at a Memorial lecture for the late Mr. SS Nadkarni, an iconic Banker and Capital market Regulator. The Keynote speaker had just completed his address. An organizer spotted Mr. Damodaran in the audience and requested if he could speak a few words, considering that the Late Mr. SS Nadkarni was also a former Chairman of SEBI. Mr. Damodaran was caught off guard. I remember he turned to me and said, tell me quickly about SS Nadkarni, his professionalism, family, his values, and his contribution to Society. I told him as I walked with him to the dais. It must have taken about 2 minutes. He was on the dais for over half an hour holding the audience spellbound as he talked on Leadership, Values, Commitment and how Institution Builders like SS Nadkarni had left their mark on the economic and industrial map of India.

Master Strategist

Mr. Damodaran moved on from IDBI in February 2005 when he was appointed as the Chairman of SEBI. His turnaround of UTI was remarkable, as he had laid the foundation which allowed IDBI to take advantage of the resurgence in the economy between 2003 to 2009. Mr. Damodaran was always able to motivate his team with the courage of his convictions. Occasionally while encouraging and motivating the staff for better performance, (being a sports fan), he would bring in snippets from the world of soccer or cricket. He was not afraid to experiment with new ideas or take calculated risks. He was able to pick the right persons for a complex job without breathing down their neck. He was firm in his convictions and did not tolerate incompetence and disloyalty. He was a master strategist, and as a scion of a very prominent industrialist family said, "it was difficult to outguess him".

Mr. Damodaran continues to contribute his knowledge and skill to some of the best corporates in the country as a Director/ Chairman and more importantly as a policy influencer in

Corporate Governance. His Articles, Round Table Conferences and Seminars give a deep sighted understanding of the complexity and interplay of today's Business, Regulation and Processes. An article written by Mr. Damodaran "From Greed to Grief" best reflects the responsibilities we all carry in the conduct of business. His contribution to the revival of IDBI will always be remembered - as an example of efficient crisis management

❑

Chapter 13

Damodaran as SEBI Chairman—A Reformer of the Indian Capital Market

– Tajinder Singh
Retd IAS

"I plead not guilty!" This used to be Mr Damodaran's response to those who would bestow on him compliments for significant accomplishments in reforming the Indian capital market as SEBI Chairman; thus demonstrating both a sense of humour and humility, one of the many endearing qualities of this intellectual giant that I had the pleasure to serve with in SEBI.

I had earlier worked in Tripura as a young Sub Divisional Officer when Mr Damodaran was the youngest Chief Secretary in the country. As head of the civil services in the state, I remember his ability to inspire fearlessness in young officers and his support in enabling them to perform to their best. He clearly demonstrated a quality that is quite rare; you always knew he had your back, thus motivating and inspiring the young ones like me.

Prior to SEBI, I had joined as Director at the Mumbai office of the Custodian under the Ministry of Finance in August 2002. This provided me an opportunity to deal with SEBI, RBI, broker-dealers, funds, exchanges, and banks. Mr Damodaran was then the Chairman of UTI. When Mr Damodaran took over as SEBI Chairman on 18 February 2005, I called on him the same evening. I waited with Katy Damania, his Secretary, before Mr Damodaran gave me a round of the Nariman Point office clearly signalling his intent to shake up SEBI – and shake up he did!

Following my tenure at the Custodian's office, I was deputed in mid-2006 by the Government to SEBI and appointed as Chief General Manager in the Integrated Surveillance Department at its Nariman Point Head Office. It was an interesting time, especially since SEBI had acquired the Integrated Market Surveillance System in what was probably one of the first few examples of the use of Supervisory Tech at the time by the capital market regulator.

Due Recognition of hard work of subordinates

After a few months in that job, Mr Damodaran called me to his office one day and asked me to draft the Prime Minister's speech for the inauguration of SEBI's new office in a few months' time in the Bandra Kurla Complex. Apparently he was happy with the draft I had produced. After that he involved me in the inauguration function including liasoning with the PM's team given that as IAS officers we gain quite some experience in handling VVIP visits. Prime Minister Manmohan Singh's speech at the inauguration of SEBI Bhavan did end up drawing quite heavily on my draft and was very well received by the media and other stakeholders. Meanwhile, Mr Damodaran also appointed me as SEBI's Head of the Office of International Affairs (OIA) ahead of the 2007 Mumbai IOSCO Annual Conference which was very unusual for an outsider like me in such an organisation.

One day Mr Damodaran called me to his office and asked if I would like to take over as his Executive Assistant (EA) once we moved to the new SEBI Headquarters. In spite of its name, the role is probably better described as Chief of Staff of the Chairman's Office.

The third role to which I was appointed following the move to SEBI Bhavan was as Head of HR; I gave up my surveillance role. In effect I had three roles in three "territories": within the building itself as Head of HR; outside India's borders as Head of the OIA; and outside the building but largely within India's borders in the Chairman's office. This was only because of the trust and confidence of Mr Damodaran - one of the qualities which distinguish him from many others in the civil services.

Extremely Competent Administrator

What followed was a very varied, exciting and satisfying stint for me in each of these three areas, and that is the multifaceted lens through which I look back at Mr Damodaran during this period - both as an extremely competent administrator professionally, and as a warm and large-hearted friend personally.

Under Mr Damodaran's leadership, we greatly revitalised the HR functioning of SEBI, amending the Regulations to provide for Campus recruitment. Mr Damodaran and I personally visited top business and law schools and interacted with the students. After I wrote to the Directors of the Indian Institutes of Management (IIMs) I remember getting a call from the Director of one of the IIMs asking us to take a reality check as to why IIM students would join public service by working as SEBI officers! Remember - these were the days of the 2007 market before the 2008 global financial crisis. Mr Damodaran's stance on this, which I reiterated in my conversation with the Director as well as in my campus visits, was that we were indeed looking for someone who would be thinking of their careers in an unconventional manner—since public service at SEBI at that time was indeed unconventional. We were not looking for dozens to join SEBI but one or two from the batch who wanted to think of a SEBI career as opposed to joining an investment bank. As in many other initiatives, Mr Damodaran's pitch was unbeatable: 'after five years would your CV not stand out compared to the rest of your batch who would have all been in some financial institution or other? And we don't want to ask you to take SEBI as your lifelong career; in fact if after 5 or 10 years you were still around in SEBI we would be asking you why?'! By amending some provisions especially around compensation in lieu of accommodation, SEBI was able to attract and retain talented young people. As a result, around 60 students from top Business and Law schools ended up joining SEBI, and I am happy to see that many of them are doing very well—some are with institutions such as the IMF and OECD and some—I am happy to say - are still with SEBI. In fact I end up meeting many of them professionally even now. Under Mr Damodaran's leadership, we also initiated a comprehensive training program for all officers: both in the country and abroad. Entire batches of officers were trained in behavioural skills with the assistance of the IIMs through one-week long residential programmes.

Very Well Recognised Internationally

On the international front, Mr Damodaran was elected as Chairman of the Emerging Markets Committee (EMC) of IOSCO in 2006. The EMC Chair, together with the Executive Committee and Technical Committee Chairs, formed the troika of IOSCO leadership in charge of key decisions. The Chair of the IOSCO Executive Committee, Jane Diplock, often used to look to him for wisdom in the middle of difficult situations.

SEBI organized the 2007 IOSCO Annual Conference which was hailed as the "Mumbai milestone". This was a great learning opportunity for me in terms of the organization of such an Annual Conference—many other countries that have hosted it describe this akin to organizing a wedding in the family! As part of the exposure of our international guests to Indian culture, Mr Damodaran had asked for a sample of the dances of India from all the different states to be presented during one of the evening functions. When the event manager showed the rehearsal to us and asked us for the sequence of dances, Mr Damodaran joked with me asking if I had ever imagined that joining the civil service would also include my "directing" a dance performance!

Effective Communicator

One aspect that has stood out in all these years of my having seen many IOSCO Annual Conferences by now is how effectively Mr Damodaran went about the communications for this event. There were newspaper articles in prominent dailies in the lead up to the Annual Conference, followed by TV interviews with the Chairman, myself and others. During the Annual Conference, there was impressive coverage both in the newspapers and on TV with interviews of many of the world's regulators.

Clear communication was also something that I was privileged to witness first hand as I went with Mr Damodaran to many of his interviews, speeches and panel discussions. He asked me to accompany him for many such engagements in Mumbai in his car, and he would ask me for some key points on the way. I now realize that this was about helping me reflect on the main issues rather than me giving him any "gyaan", though he did mention some of these points during his speeches. His clear thinking and direct style made him pretty much a darling of the media.

Complete 'Market' Man

The number of achievements in SEBI is too numerous to list out, so here is a flavour of a few: Corporatisation and Demutualisation of all 18 Indian Stock Exchanges, Derivative Market reforms, Corporate Governance reforms of listed companies through the listing rules, strengthening surveillance through the Integrated

Market Surveillance System, giving greater teeth to enforcement through disgorgement orders, introduction of short selling rules and securitization regulations, reduction of mutual fund expenses and simplified issuance of debt among others. Development of the capital markets themselves, in addition to their regulation—or rather through introducing enabling regulation that set the guardrails for the healthy development of these markets—was a key priority for Mr Damodaran. While being a healthy sceptic of the lobbying by financial institutions including some global players, he was nonetheless a believer in building a "complete" market—hence the emphasis on topics that could be seen as controversials like short selling, introduction of derivatives, securitization etc. These were before the days of the smartphone, but that did not hold back Mr Damodaran in being super-fast in his responses to staff using SMS's—some called it Regulation by SMS!

In his interactions with the Government, he was always courteous but was acutely conscious of the need for the autonomy of SEBI, both in substantive and perception terms. He was clear that he would not accept SEBI being seen by some as a subordinate or attached office of the Government. That, of course, meant some difficult conversations with the Government but at the root of it was not an ego trip, rather one of ensuring that SEBI is seen as a trusted and respected regulator both domestically and globally, which was crucial for investors' confidence—something that Mr Damodaran was able to achieve in no small measure.

One of Mr Damodaran's brilliant initiatives was the setting up of the National Institute of Securities Markets (NISM) which was incubated as part of the Chairman's office by another outstanding Tripura cadre (ex-)IAS officer, Prof G Sethu. Starting from the creation of the project plan to the building of the campus to the running of training programmes (even before the campus was built) was truly impressive. The number of donors who wanted to have a piece of the action was as interesting as the strategy which got them in: instead of courting the donors, Mr Damodaran made it clear that there was a finite window within which they needed to make up their minds whether or not they wanted to donate towards the cause of a national training institute sponsored by SEBI—while of course making sure that any conflicts of interest were addressed. This led to a phenomenon where donors were chasing us asking to extend the timeline, rather than the other way round.

On a personal note, being able to work so closely with Mr Damodaran gave me many moments worth treasuring. He was always kind to me and even in the presence of Chairmen and CEOs he would describe me as his conscience keeper. I fondly remember the innumerable cups of tea throughout the day in his room in the course of dealing with many difficult issues; joining Mr Damodaran at lunch in the 8th floor Executive Dining room or in his private dining room; and his affectionately calling me over to his office in the late evenings for a *masala dosa*. When finally leaving office, he would ask me to accompany him in his Toyota Sumo while I enjoyed his reflections on the day as he dropped me home on the way to the Chairman's residence. I also remember accompanying him for the first time to an IOSCO Executive Committee meeting at the IOSCO Headquarters in Madrid where he pointed out the Bernabeu stadium as the mecca of football: little did I know that I would be living in this city for the next many years working for IOSCO!

'Sachin Tendulkar' of the Financial Sector

Mr Damodaran's three year tenure ended in February 2008—it was clearly short in arithmetical terms but by no means in achievement. I can do no better than quote from his letter to the Prime Minister on 18 Feb 2008, his last day in office:

"...twelve and a half years ago in August 1996, reportedly against the advice of senior Ministry officials, you had brought to the Ministry of Finance as Joint Secretary, a relatively anonymous

officer from Tripura. In the twelve and a half years gone by, I have had the opportunity to deal with several aspects of, and institutions in, the financial sector. A brief stint with the Reserve Bank of India enabled me to contribute to the restructuring efforts of three weak public sector banks. Thereafter, I had the unique challenge and opportunity to restructure India's largest mutual fund, the then ailing Unit Trust of India. Later I undertook the long pending merger of IDBI and IDBI Bank Ltd, to address the myriad problems that both of them faced. Three years ago I was given the responsibility of heading SEBI. During this period the Indian securities market has grown significantly and has seen new products and better processes. Internationally there is considerable respect for, and recognition of, the regulatory standards in our markets, and my Chairmanship of the 80 member Emerging Markets Committee of IOSCO is perhaps evidence of that recognition.

Today, I leave the SEBI building which you kindly inaugurated at my request a little over a year ago. I had then thanked you for giving SEBI a new home and described SEBI as your own child. As I embark on a new phase of my life I would like to believe that the officer you brought from the North East into the Ministry of Finance, leading later to opportunities in RBI, UTI, IDBI and SEBI might have done enough to be worthy of your continuing affection."

This in brief summarises Mr Damodaran tenure in the financial sector - He left a mark in the institutions he worked with and built a 'lobby' of officers who are and continue to be obliged to him throughout their life in view of the guidance, motivation, encouragement and personal affection extended by him officially or otherwise. With his love for sports, he can be truly called the "Sachin Tendulkar " of the Indian financial sector, especially the capital market.

❑

Chapter 14

A Unique Personality—Perspective from Younger Generation

– Divyani Garg

It was in February 2009 that a Professor of mine in Masters had told me that he had given my name as reference to Mr M Damodaran, former Chairman of SEBI. This was in connection with Mr Damodaran's requirement to hire an HR professional to assist in his new endeavour. In March 2009 when I received a call from an unknown mobile number (truecaller was not an app then), I definitely did not expect Mr Damodaran to be on the other side of the line. He had called me to check whether I was available for a chat the following day, in his office located at Jaisingh Road, New Delhi. He took the extra pain of explaining to me the location, as also the possible route that I should consider taking from my home. What truly floored me was his saying that he had a lunch appointment, and he might be late by 5 minutes, and in case that was to be, I should wait for him. He also apologised for that in advance. In this day and age, when traffic and "Indian Standard Time" are par for the course, here was a man, so senior to me, such an achiever, giving value to 5 minutes of my time. The "interview" turned out to be a fun chat, where he told me what he wanted to do post his superannuation, and mentioned that he was going to visit his mother in Chennai the following day, and would call me once he returned. I did get that call a week later, and he asked me to come the following day, which was, as I later discovered, the day I started working with him. No letter of appointment, no conversation about designation or salary, or even a properly drawn out job description. I went with my gut feeling, and I am so glad that I did.

In college, we all read about the qualities of a leader. I am not exaggerating when I say that after knowing, and working, with Mr Damodaran for over a decade, that list is not complete. Here is a man, who I have had the privilege of knowing, working with, and being mentored by, for over 14 years. There are far too many seemingly inconsequential qualities about him, which make a person fond of him. I come from a background where no one in my family has worked in the Government. I did have some notions. He has single handedly quashed each one of them. He once asked me why I had never thought of IAS as an option. I had told him "that is because I had never met you before". And I had meant it.

In no particular order, I have tried to list down some of the traits that make him unique. Anyone, aspiring to be a leader, should give some consideration to these. This is truly the equivalent of "what they do not teach you in MBA schools".

Humility

For a person who has achieved so much in life, there has never been a day where he has bossed around anyone, irrespective of where the person is in the hierarchy. He believes in being the same, not letting the designation of the person decide his behaviour. I once asked him why people were scared to retire. His response was that it was because when they ring the bell on their table, there is no one on the other side to answer it and that scares people. I asked him why that never bothered him. His response was classically him. I like to be self-dependent, and of course there is Neeraj (our office boy).

Building Institutions

How many persons can boast of rescuing institutions, and building them, such that long after their demitting office, the institution flourishes and continues to grow? It is unimaginable how a person who grew up in Kerala/ Tamil Nadu, was at peace going to Tripura. Not once, but thrice. He not only learnt the local language and became popular with the locals, but also went on to become the Chief Secretary. It is unimaginable how he convinced RBI to make him OSD in Delhi, because he did not want to relocate to Mumbai. It is unimaginable how he unquestioningly took over as CMD of UTI and later as CMD of IDBI concurrently (as though his workload in UTI was less), given the state these institutions were in, during that time. He did enough for Tripura's budgets by taking the State's finances from a situation of overdraft, to being recognised and rewarded, for financial management. He ensured some public sector banks were rescued (and they all thrive even today) when he was associated with MOF and RBI. Of course, UTI and IDBI continue to grow as organisations. As the shortest tenured Chairman of SEBI, he ensured that other securities commissions sat up, and took note of SEBI. His election as Chairman of IOSCO's 80 member Emerging Markets Committee is testimony to this. This was in addition to all that he did to protect Indian markets. He truly believes in building institutions. While working with him, I have also seen him become the first Chair of one of the newer IIMs, IIM Tiruchirappalli. He ensured that not only did the institute get a good Director, but he reached out to the Ministry several times for help. He also ensured that the foundation stone for the campus was laid while he was the Chairman, so that the campus itself becomes a source of pride for students in the future.

Benevolence

He is one of the kindest persons I have known. I have yet to come across a person who has reached out to him for help, and has not received it. He always says that if he is fortunate enough to help people, he must do so. There are persons from different walks of life, some of whom he does not even know. All they do is send him mail, and if he can help, he does so. He can never be seen publicly even mentioning any act of kindness that he might have done for another person.

People's Person

He continues to remind all those who would hear that he never pursued Masters. However, he is a true "people's person". He truly believes that organizations are differentiated on the basis of the people who work there. In all institutions that he has been associated with, there are enough and more incidents which will show what he did for people (employees), that most heads of organizations would not do. From granting maternity leave to an unmarried woman in 1976 on the ground that health and not marital status was important, to launching HR schemes where people could own houses in Mumbai because their HRA was increased, to introducing the practice of getting middle level persons to have lunch with their Chairman as a token of his appreciation for their efforts, there are any number of incidents, big or small, that people who have worked with him will narrate. People, across genders, have reached out to him when in distress, and he has never let them down. No one can dispute the fact that he is very approachable. Despite the positions that he has held, he carries his achievements very lightly on his shoulders. Giving credit to his team, and not taking credit, comes to him naturally.

Integrity

He was, is and will always be honest to the core. He has always taught people around him that honesty and self-respect, under any circumstances, is non-negotiable. He keeps telling people, especially young people, that "distance from greed to grief, in the dictionary, is only a few pages." He has been honest to admit when he was wrong, or even about incidents like why he ran away from IIT. In the era when he did, leaving the IIT was surely a scandal, yet ex-IITians continue to reach out to him, and call him one of their own.

Patience

He is not one to lose his cool (unless someone has really gone out of his/her way to ensure so). He jokingly says that losing his cool would mean that he had lost something. He has been through some of the toughest meetings with persons who were not well disposed to him. He has been extremely patient in the way he has approached these meetings.

Punctuality

I have often heard him say, to be late is disrespectful to the other person. He has hardly even been late for meetings, and if he is stuck, he is the first person to call and inform.

Realistic and Pragmatic

Working with him is not tough. His ground rules are simple. Be honest to your work, and if you make a mistake, there is no problem but do not repeat it. He never has unrealistic expectations from anyone who works with him, and would encourage one and all to perform to their potential. Excellence Enablers, a company founded by Mr Damodaran, had once hosted a talk show with senior persons from the industry and some students in Mumbai. I was overall in-charge of the arrangements. There was some big mistake with the backdrop, which impacted the overall look of the venue, and could have caused some issues with the show's sponsors. I was very upset. All he said was it was not your mistake, and these things happen. He has never even raised this topic ever after.

Great Orator

His speeches are works of art. He is not one to speak to a script. Impromptu speeches, complete with relevant incidents and stories, makes everyone want to keep hearing him. Even when he goes as a member of the audience, there have been occasions when he has been asked to come to the stage and address the audience. It is interesting how he has never said no, and has always had some anecdote or story to liven up the mood. A couple of months ago, we went to one of the big CA firms in India, where he was asked to address the parents of newly inducted CAs. It was fun to see how he had the audience in splits. In fact, one of the Partners there fondly remembered how Mr Damodaran had given a speech at his college, and quoted a couple of sentences from that speech. Such is the impact of his speeches on the audiences.

Remembering Persons by Name

All stories and incidents that he narrates, going back to when he was a probationer with State Bank of India, and even before, does not just have people, but each of those persons has a name. He has made it his business to remember everyone's names. I have seen people's mouths open in awe when he has addressed them by name, because they were almost certain that he would not remember.

Empathy

While sympathy is easy to come by, here is a man, who genuinely is empathetic to people and their needs. He is the last person to judge, and the first to give another person the benefit of the doubt, because he can empathise with the person and the circumstances that the other may be in.

Not Hierarchically Driven

Ours is a funny organisation, in the sense that I report to him, with almost 40 years between us. Never in the last over 14 years have I felt him dismiss any thought or idea or concern that I may have expressed because I am much younger. On the contrary, he has been so supportive and encouraging, that a lot of our offerings in the past have been a mix of both our "over the top" thinking, thereby challenging us to deliver. I have met enough and more people who have worked with him in Tripura, UTI, IDBI and SEBI, and the one thing that is common is that he enjoys affection from each one of them because he has always cut across ranks, and never restricted himself to people who were his "direct reportees/ colleagues". He encourages people irrespective of their age, and is always willing to patiently listen to their points of view.

Non-judgemental

He keeps quoting Sridevi from "English Vinglish" for when she said one must not be judgemental. Even before she said so, he was never guilty of judging anyone. He truly believes that every coin has two sides, and one must not jump the gun and judge.

Leading with Example

Management books would always use words such as "lead with example", "setting the tone at the top" and the like. Given the senior positions that he has held, it is impossible to believe that there were no pressures on him to perform contrary to what he did. However, without probably even realising so, he has led by example, not always taking the easier way out. He has always had the back of people who have worked with him, and who too were under pressure, despite being on the straight and narrow path of truthfulness.

Well-informed

I jokingly call him my google and my grammar teacher. He is one of the most well-read persons. Not only does he read, he has the ability to remember what he has read. He has never restricted himself to reading about some specific topics only. The range, the depth, and the quality of his knowledge is the stuff that human Wikipedias are made of. Along with this, he reads in excess of 10 newspapers a day, and when he is travelling abroad, the one recurring thing that he misses is his daily newspapers. He has the perfect explanation, example, anecdote or reference to give to anyone seeking information from him. Listening to his stories is a delight. His command over the English language has always made everyone admire his writings. The patience with which he removes errors such as "of" from "comprise of", is truly admirable.

Patience of A Teacher

There are 3 alternate careers that he would have excelled at. Being a teacher, being a lawyer, and being associated with the advertising industry. He is extremely patient while teaching or explaining any concept to anyone. I had joined him as a fresher, with not even the foggiest idea of a concept called "Corporate Governance". Whatever I know today, is all due to him. In his own way, he made me read law, regulations, books, articles, insights... the list is long.. to make me who I am today. As for being a lawyer, his interpretation of sections and regulations has made General Counsels of some of the largest companies in India sit up. Writing ad copy is something that comes naturally to him. Some of the ads of UTI were his own creation.

Staying Relevant

He is one of the few who have very smoothly transitioned from being a hard core Government person to now working mostly with the private sector. The Boards that he sits on, the companies that he is associated with, have been possible because he constantly works on himself for being relevant. He believes in adapting, in upgrading, and in just moving with the current times. I once saw him read an urban dictionary because he wanted to get the meaning of a slang. I was impressed. Post superannuation (as against retirement), his accomplishment of setting up on his own, to be on Boards of some of the largest companies in India, to be associated with some international organisations,must all be credited to his upgrading himself. He loves to read on a variety of topics, interact with persons from different backgrounds, and browse the internet on the latest trends.

Out of the Box Solutions

He has always taught me to come to him with a solution, and not a problem. It is easy to find faults with something. But when you are in the driver's seat, it may not be easy to come up with an alternate or a solution. He has always believed in having creative solutions. One of the ways to do so, that he always advises, is to look for the space between what is prescribed and what is proscribed, and find a solution in that space. Believe me, it always works. In a world of sensational media and stories, he has always believed and taught that focus should be on issues and not people. If one is to truly find solutions, issues and not people, are important. From increasing HRA in UTI so that people working in the organisation could buy their own houses in the city of Mumbai to the restructuring of UTI and IDBI, which is much spoken of even today, to making the then-SEBI financially independent, none of his solutions fit the "one solution fits all approach".

Time Management

In over 14 years that I have worked with him, his own style of time management has always amazed me. Work wise no two days are identical. There are pressures of various kinds. He ensures that his mental bandwidth expands to accommodate the quantity of work, as also the diversity of it, such that it is completed in record time. While he might have a fixed time for reaching office, there have often been occasions when both of us have worked without seeing the clock.

Listen to Others

He often credits most of his success to his ability to listen to others. He always says God has given us two ears and one mouth. They should be used in that proportion. He has always encouraged persons working with him to give ideas or solutions to problems, and is never dismissive of any idea. When he was the Chairperson of IIM Tiruchirappalli, he was the happiest person interacting with students, and listening to their experiences in Tiruchirappalli. No wonder, he is at ease interacting with people of all ages.

Work-life Balance

While he has never been a practitioner of work-life balance, he surely is a family man. I have had the privilege and honour of meeting his mother, and the only thing that she was concerned about was his not taking care of his health in the process of work being more important than personal life. Conversations on similar grounds with Ma'am (Mrs Damodaran) or his two sons, also lead to the same conclusion. He does not look after himself. When not travelling, his way of destressing is movies, and for a man with insurmountable amounts of patience, he loves action movies. He truly believes that hobbies are important.

The list is long. To compress 14 years of learnings into a couple of pages is impossible if the person you are tasked to write about is Mr Damodaran. Suffice it to say, so many people, across organisations, sectors, and age groups, look up to him, for reasons more than one because he is truly unique. Clearly a sign of a true leader- qualities he possesses need to be emphasized in all management schools and for all those joining the civil services.

❑

Contributors

1. **Dinesh Kumar Tyagi –** An IAS officer of Manipur- Tripura cadre. Worked as secretary education, tribal welfare and finance in the State of Tripura. Worked as Director in the banking Division Ministry of Finance and as custodian of Harshad Mehta scam. Went on deputation to IL&FS as CEO of the CSC project. Resigned from IAS in 2008. Worked as CEO and MD of the CSC SPV – a company promoted by Ministry of electronics and IT, GOI till the year 2022
2. **Dr K Cherian Varghese –** Joined as an officer in the Indian bank. worked in Indian Bank in various capacities. Joined as ED of Central Bank and CMD in corporation bank and Union bank of India. Became the chairman of the BIFR
3. **Rehman Imtaiyazur –** worked in UTI in various capacities
4. **Sushil Kumar –** An IAS officer of Manipur-Tripura cadre. Worked in various capacities in the State as Director, secretary Animal husbandry etc. Was Secretary to Government of India – Ministry of Mines Retired as Secretary to the SC commission
5. **Dr V K Bahuguna –** An IFS officer of Manipur-Tripura cadre. Worked in various capacities in the state as DFO, conservator etc. Worked in Ministry of Forest and Environment GOI and later as Director General Indian Council of Forestry Research and Education Dehradun. Has more than 200 publications in forest and related matters. Is a prolific writer – on various topics on national interest

6. **Rajeshwar Rao** - An IAS officer of Manipur-Tripura cadre. Worked as secretary to Chief Minister and in various other departments as Secretary in the State. Worked in the erstwhile state of Andhra Pradesh on deputation as secretary urban development. Was Additional Secretary in the Ministry of Mines GOI. Worked as Advisor to Niti Ayog GOI

7. **Dr Sabahat Azim** - An IAS officer of Manipur-Tripura cadre. Worked as Secretary to Chief Minister. Later resigned and set up "Glocal "– a low cost health care service provider company which was listed on the New York Stock exchange and also set up such health facilities in many countries across the world

8. **G Sethu** - An IAS officer of Manipur- Tripura cadre. Worked as Director Industries and in other capacities in the State. Resigned and joined as faculty at the UTI Institute of Capital Markets. Later set up the National Institute of Capital Market and worked as its founder Director. Worked as a Director at the IIM Tiruchirappalli.

9. **Dr A K Krishna Kumar** – worked in the Rubber Board in various capacities as Joint director etc. Implemented the Rubber based rehabilitation project for tribals in Tripura. Joined IL&FS cluster and designed and developed many unique projects as Bamboo cluster, agri based cluster etc

10. **Anil Parasher** – in Indigo as director

11. **MBN Rao** – joined as an officer in Indian Bank. Worked as GM, ED and later CMD of the Indian Bank and Canara Bank. Was associated with the revival and restructuring of the Indian Bank. Associated with various committees set up by Government for setting up ARC, legislative reforms etc. Former Chairman of Indian Banks Associations.

12. **Jitender Balakrishnan** – worked in various capacities in IDBI including as ED

13. **Tajinder Singh -** An IAS officer of Manipur- Tripura cadre. Worked in various capacities in the State Government. As Director in the Ministry of Finance, GOI in the office of the custodian (Harshad Mehta scam). Joined in SEBI and worked as the OSD to chairman. Joined ICOSOC and is presently working there based at Sweden

14. **Divyani Garg** – working in Excellence enabler – an organization set up by Mr Damodaran.

❑❑

Meleveetil Damodaran (Ex IAS)

Chairperson, Excellence Enablers Private Limited
Former Chairman, Securities and Exchange Board of India (SEBI), Unit Trust of India (UTI) & Industrial Development Bank of India (IDBI)

Meleveetil Damodaran belongs to 1971 batch of Indian Administrative Service. In his career spanning over 52 years, he has worked with the Union and the State governments in India, regulatory bodies, investment institutions, banks, development financial institutions and with the private sector. Beside working in various capacities in the State of Tripura , he was appointed as its Chief Secretary in 1992, the youngest ever in the country to hold such a position in any State Government. As Chief electoral officer, In addition to being the chief secretary , and under quite hostile circumstances , he conducted the State Assembly elections without a single instance of repoll and without a single election related death.

He worked as Joint Secretary in the Ministry of Finance, Banking Division, for five years, dealing with Government's ownership functions of Public Sector Banks and being its interface with Reserve Bank of India (RBI), the regulator of India's banking system. Thereafter, as Officer on Special Duty with RBI, he co-ordinated the revival plans for three identified weak public sector banks, Indian Bank, UCO Bank and United Bank of India, the closure of which had been recommended by CII in a report on banking.

In 2001, he was appointed the Chairman of Unit Trust of India (UTI) to rescue India's largest and oldest investment institution which had collapsed. His restoring of UTI to health and strength is widely acknowledged as the most successful turnaround story in India's Financial Sector. An institution whose obituary had been written was restructured as India's largest mutual fund with exemplary governance practices being put in place. He was simultaneously given charge of Industrial Development Bank of India (IDBI), another of India's major financial institutions, which too was restructured by him in an innovative manner, pulling it back from the brink, transforming it to a bank, and merging it with another commercial bank.

As Chairman SEBI, he brought improved practices to India's securities market. He is widely acknowledged as one of the India's foremost champions of Corporate Governance. During his tenure at SEBI, he was elected Chairman of the International Organization of Securities Commissions (IOSCO)'s 80 member Emerging Markets Committee for two years.

He is presently an Independent Director on the Boards of Larsen and Toubro, and Biocon. Till recently, he served as an Independent Director on the Boards of CRISIL, Tech Mahindra and Hero MotoCorp. He served as the non-executive Chairperson of InterGlobe Aviation (IndiGo) for 3 years. He is a Nominee Director on the Boards of InterGlobe Aviation (IndiGo), Bajaj Allianz General Insurance Company and Bajaj Allianz Life Insurance Company. He was also Advisor and Chief Representative in India for the ING Group of Netherlands.

He is the founder of Excellence Enablers, a specialist Corporate Governance initiative that focuses on improvement of Board performance and addresses emerging needs of corporate India. He was the founder Chairman of the Society and Board of Governors of the Indian Institute of Management Tiruchirappalli (IIMT). He also chaired the Government of India

Committee for suggesting amendments to laws and regulations for Venture Capital and Private Equity investments.

Within the Civil Service he is considered as a "Role Model" and in the financial sector "Highly Innovative Institutional Revival Person"

He has been a recipient of several prestigious awards for leadership, transformation and Public Service.

List of some Awards

1. Life Time Achievement Award in Ethical Governance and Leadership by Asian Centre for Corporate Governance and Sustainability (2015)
2. Life Time Achievement Award in Public Governance by Asian Centre for Corporate Governance and Sustainability (2013)
3. Policy Change Agent of the Year (2006-07) by Economic Times
4. India Business Leaders Award (2006) for Outstanding Contribution to the Cause of Indian Business by CNBC
5. Public Service Excellence Award (2009) by All India Management Association
6. Finance Man of the Year (2004) by Bombay Management Association, Association of Leasing and Financial Service Companies of India, Association of Merchant Bankers of India, Association of Mutual Funds in India, Finance Industry Development Council, Indian Merchant's Chambers and Institute of Chartered Financial Analysts of India
7. National Award for Outstanding Contribution in the Field of Public Service (2004) by Priyadarshini Academy at their 20th Anniversary Global Awards Function

❑